Christopher Alexander and the Eishin Campus

SHIFTING PATTERNS

Christopher Alexander and the Eishin Campus

Edited by Eva Guttmann,
Gabriele Kaiser, Claudia Mazanek

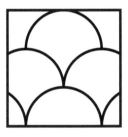

PARK BOOKS

63–123
Eishin Campus and site plan
Photographs by Helmut Tezak

Eight Haikus
by Ferdinand Schmatz

Contents

11
Eva Guttmann, Gabriele Kaiser
"What we see—and what we understand"

22
Ernst Beneder
Tokyo, 1984

40
Walter Ruprechter
On the Cultural Ambiguity of the Eishin Campus

50
Hisae Hosoi
"Sweet Home in My Heart"

124
Hajo Neis (Conversation)
Shifting Values in Architecture and Urban Design

143
Christian Kühn
The Pattern Language for the Eishin Campus

151
Ida Pirstinger
Urban Order and the Ambivalence of the Patterns

161
Norihito Nakatani
Why Recall Christopher Alexander?

166
Takaharu Tezuka (Conversation)
"Sometimes inconvenience is luxury."

178 Biography and Bibliography

Eva Guttmann, Gabriele Kaiser
"What we see—and what we understand."

Who wouldn't appreciate houses that convince people by their naturalness and "timelessness?" On the other hand: Doesn't the appeal to archetypes in architecture all too easily come close to a backward-looking reconciliation with a world whose unmanageability is lamented in references to the "good old days that are critical of civilization?" Does the attempt to confront the profit-driven construction industry with something more alive, more humane and more diverse than the norm of the built find its place in architectural history at best as a poetic utopia?

Questions like these emerged when we reflected upon the idea of dedicating a book to the Vienna-born architect and planning theorist Christopher Alexander. His major published work, *A Pattern Language: Towns, Buildings, Construction* (first edition in 1977), may be well known and appreciated, but the use of this language is not. Apart from the books he edited and published himself, there is no monographic literature on Christopher Alexander's architectural oeuvre. In Austria, perhaps the "Linz Café," built as part of the Forum Design exhibition in 1980, is a term some are familiar with. Journal articles from the 1980s give a vague idea of the largest project Christopher Alexander was able to realize with the Center for Environmental Structure (CES) at the University of California, Berkeley—the Eishin Campus near Tokyo. In 2012, Alexander presented a bitter chronicle of the Eishin Campus's planning and construction process, *The Battle for the Life and Beauty of the Earth. A Struggle Between Two World-Systems,* in which he recounted the project's successes and upheavals while sharply criticizing the practices of "investor architecture": Good against evil, "System A" (the ordinary way of building) versus "System B" (mechanistic building)—"a struggle between two world-systems …" What makes this book so special is the mixture of the meticulous documentation of a formation process, the "reckoning" with those who sought to undermine the Alexandrine concept from his point of view, and an emphatic appeal to return to basic human needs when building.

Although the book leaves an ambiguous impression behind, the uniqueness of the built project remains in memory, arouses our curiosity and ultimately the desire to re-document the Campus as a type of applied Pattern Language around 30 years after its completion, and to exemplarily investigate the timeliness and universality of Alexander's theories. Above all, we are interested in the question as to whether and how the Pattern Language or a specific "Project Language" proves itself in practical application, and which dynamic force an architecture understood as living could develop. The theme of transfer between the European-American and the Asian cultural spheres should likewise be touched upon—a new reading and gleaning which the chosen book title *Shifting Patterns* also refers to.

This attempt also seems worthwhile to us inasmuch as the interest in elementary and simple building has moved into the middle of architectural discourse since the 1990s with the resurgence of the design-build movement and is now experiencing a broader reception. In this context, the architectural and theoretical work of Christopher Alexander would deserve a rediscovery, especially as the appreciation of a naturally grown building culture beyond the formalistic canon of Modernism had already found a critical basis in Austria in the early 20th century through architects like Adolf Loos and Josef Frank. In his essay *"Christopher Alexander und die Wiener Moderne"* ("Christopher Alexander and Viennese Modernism"), Hermann Czech outlined the conceptual context, naturally without postulating an explicit elective affinity.[1]

Under quite different auspices, generic architecture in Austria and the fascination with an unconscious, collective form finding experienced a boom in the 1960s, such as in Roland Rainer's study *Anonymes Bauen Nordburgenland* (1961), Traude Windbrechtinger's essay *"Anonyme Architektur"* (1961), Hans Hollein's lecture *"Zurück*

[1] Hermann Czech, "Christopher Alexander und die Wiener Moderne," *ARCH+* 73, March 1984, 63–65; English in Hermann Czech, *Essays on Architecture and City Planning*, trans. Elise Feiersinger, Zurich: Park Books, 2019.

zur Architektur" (1962), Raimund Abraham's *Elementare Architektur* (1963), Bernard Rudofsky's exhibition and book *Architecture Without Architects* (1964), or in Günther Feuerstein's *Archetypen des Bauens* (1967). Carl Pruscha's long-standing preoccupation with vernacular architecture in the Himalayan region could also be mentioned in this connection.

The mathematician and architect Christopher Alexander occupies a special position in the context of those just mentioned. He was already concerned in the 1960s with much more than the rehabilitation of anonymous architecture or an archaic reference for one's own work outside the mainstream. After his dissertation *Notes on the Synthesis of Form* (1964), Alexander presented a collection of design patterns for the simple "making of buildings" in the late 1970s with his methodological foundational work *A Pattern Language*, which essentially includes the volume *A Timeless Way of Building* as well. *A Pattern Language* moreover addressed aspects of settlement and urban planning, offering a universally understood pattern language made up of 253 freely combinable patterns based on tried-and-tested solutions that were to enable all people to design their own surroundings themselves. With this empowerment of the users, going far beyond the usual instrument of participation, Alexander seemed to have his finger on the pulse. His return to architectural archetypes and his fundamental criticism of industrialized construction was discussed heftily as well as controversially in the professional world—a controversy that probably reached its climax in the 1984 conversation between Peter Eisenman and Christopher Alexander.[2] And yet: Although *A Pattern Language* is one of the best-selling architectural books of the 20th century, celebrated as a milestone in other disciplines such as software development, it has remained an insider tip and a marginal phenomenon within architecture. Added to this is the almost complete blinding out of the architectural work: Even though Alexander was received worldwide in the 1980s, there is hardly any secondary literature that deals extensively with his buildings. Among other things, this is because Alexander reserved the right to document the conception and implementation processes of his designs.

A central aspect in the preparation of this book was the trip to Tokyo, which Helmut Tezak accompanied us on to photographically document the Eishin Campus in its present form. While the pictures from the 1980s still show the area in the midst of fields and tea plantations,

2

"DIscord Over Harmony in Architecture: The Eisenman/Alexander Debate," *HGSD News*, May–June, 1983, 5, Vol.11, 12–17.

The Campus surroundings, Iruma-shi, Saitama Prefecture

today it is surrounded by mostly (still) low development and, although located in the neighboring province of Saitama, has become part of the borderless periphery of Tokyo. The impression of an almost unreal island, which is already visible from a greater distance on account of the topography, persists when entering the area—first through the small gate and then through the main gate. Structurally remaining a torso because plans for an integrated college have been scuttled, the school campus appears multifaceted and spacious in its entirety. Reality is brought into line with the notion that we already have of the complex; the architecture awakens associations from all directions, across eras, styles and cultures. What appeals to us or raises questions varies with the view we cast on the constructive and ornamental features of the buildings. We dive into a world where aimless wandering is recommended; whichever way we go, the succession of dense and wide spaces remains surprising. Absorbed by the atmosphere of the "interstices," which open up again and again in the village-like structure, we experience the liveliness of this place, although the Campus itself—our tour takes place during the semester break—is nearly deserted.

The visits to the Campus, the encounters with conversation partners in Japan and Vienna, as well as our own impressions on site strengthened us in the wish to gather authors and interview partners from both cultures together for the book and to show the greatest possible diversity of approaches to do justice to the complexity and ambivalence of this exceptional construction project.

From left to right: Gabriele Kaiser, Minami Miyashita (translator), Yoko Kitamura (head of the school), Eva Guttmann

Taking central stage is the photographic interpretation of the complex in its present state; it forms the visual focal point and is surrounded by reflections that draw wide circles emanating from the concrete case study of the Eishin Campus. In terms of content, the arch spans from the atmospheric depiction of the metropolis of Tokyo in the 1980s, to interviews with project participants, all the way to the urban planning background and Alexander's reception in Japan in the 2000s. On one hand, the association space staked out seeks to open new accesses to the work of Christopher Alexander and, on the other hand, to reflect upon the ambivalence of his buildings and writings in the sense of a critical discussion. The respect and seriousness with which the authors approach their respective themes contributes significantly to the fact that this book functions like a kaleidoscope that reveals an object in its different facets and invites us to encounter

The English teacher Takashi Matsuura in front of the Judo Hall

Path to the classrooms

architectural particularities far from the canon in an unbiased manner. Haikus by the poet Ferdinand Schmatz, who lived in Tokyo for a few years, finally bring—while leaving everything open—"what we see" and "what we understand" to the point.

The book moves from the general to the special and back again. Architect Ernst Beneder provides the opening with his text *"Tokyo, 1984."* Beneder personally witnessed the architectural changes of that era—in a city that "increasingly considered itself as unique among the metropolitan regions," which was also perceived in the West that way. He traces an arc from the Metabolists of the 1960s, Expo '70 in Osaka, as well as Kenneth Frampton's lecture on *"Critical Regionalism"* at the GA Gallery, to the "small constructs" of Tadao Ando, Toyo Ito and Kazuo Shinohara, as well as the question of understanding *Japanese-ness* in Japan itself and in the West. It is not what is built that holds the city together, but a "consensus" that can be found "in the social code, in the disposition to the integration into the common." It is a dense, atmospheric description of the architectural positions of this time that seemingly has nothing to do with the parallel construction of the Eishin Campus. Nevertheless, connections between the Campus and passages in Beneder's text could be found: When he writes of the grammar that is to be detected in Japanese architecture, when he speaks of tolerance, basic trust and the unexpected quality of life which Tokyo, this "loud, hideous hodgepodge" according to Bruno Taut, has to offer. Perhaps there is a key to the question of how "Japanese" the Eishin Campus is, even though the relevance of this query diminishes the more one delves into the project: Both Tokyo and the Eishin Campus represent a practice of living together, the significance of which is even greater than that of the built manifestation, whereby the (urban) spatial complexity beyond the scale and the individual structure nonetheless significantly determines this practice.

Walter Ruprechter, a longtime professor of literature and cultural studies at the Tokyo Metropolitan University, covers the topic of cultural coding and analyzes possible overlaps between the Japanese building tradition and the genesis of the Eishin Campus. He begins by stating that the Campus is a project "realized by an Austro-American architectural visionary […] with a Japanese school visionary […] in Japan," and, despite the Alexandrine dichotomy between good and evil that initially blocks out intercultural factors, a principle ignoring of these factors cannot be assumed, since cultural specifics are already incorporated into every project through the method of participation alone. The author proves the existence of Japanese elements through an exact study of details and concludes that "the cultural coding, therefore, is probably also associated with the apperception, which, in turn, is culturally coded itself." Finally, Walter Ruprechter returns once more to the methodology of Christopher Alexander, in which he sees a relationship in the general conduct of the Japanese, striking a nerve that explains the importance of Alexander in Japan—in the field of architecture as well as in the critique of rationalism.

Hisae Hosoi at Café Almond, Tokyo

In a long conversation we were able to hold with Hisae Hosoi, the school principal back then and the initiator of the Eishin Campus who now lives in Malaysia, he puts some of what is to be read in *The Battle for the Life and Beauty of the Earth* into perspective. Despite all the difficulties involved in the project, Hosoi speaks with admiration and affection of "Chris," and that the design and implementation of the Eishin Campus was "the best time of [his] life." When we asked him to write a message of greetings for our book, he agreed. His voice—along with that of Hajo Neis—is one that can directly convey the formation process of the Eishin Campus. Hosoi explains the prehistory of the project, the lengthy search for an architect who understands and shares his ideas of a contemporary school as a "house to live in" and as a "place of sweet memories." To put his own ideas of a school in concrete terms, he had read a lot and had traveled just as much. He recounts the failures he had to endure before he came across Alexander through the book *The Oregon Experiment* and finally found the partner whom he could start planning the campus with. Hosoi and Alexander agreed on the importance of the processual, the rejection of formal Modernist architecture, and the role crafts and Japanese building traditions should play in this project. In detail, Hosoi describes the participatory development of the "Project Language" and ends at the point where the position of the individual buildings on the campus was completed by laying out bamboo sticks with little flags in different colors across the tea fields of the site and the construction work could begin.

Following Hosoi's account is the photographic documentation featuring pictures by Helmut Tezak. From the abundance of shots that could each tell a story on its own, we have put together a sequence that traces a "walk" through the Campus. The fact that this does not proceed in a linear mannner has to do with the intricate

THAT WHICH WE DO SEE·
IS THAT WHICH WE UNDERSTAND·
PICTURES, WORDS, PLACES·

私たちが「見る」ものは
私たちが「わかる」ものだ。
イメージ、言葉、場所。

circulation, with the numerous possibilities of accessing the area, with the complex network of references, vistas, connections and scales characerizing the complex. And indeed, the photographs show—even more than in the site plan—that there are no meaningless leftover areas on the site, that the variety of spatial situations and moods is the actual quality of the Campus.

The interview with Hajo Neis, architect and philosopher, close associate of Christopher Alexander, project manager on the Eishin Campus and current director of CES, takes place in his German hometown of Borken. We learn the background and details—not only about his collaboration with Alexander and the Eishin Campus, but also concerning the present and the future of the CES. He answers our pre-written questions in great detail, adds to topics he believes are important, and thus takes on a position that complements as well as carries forward the *Battle* and Hisae Hosoi's remarks. Through his descriptions, it becomes clear in what complex manner the principle of process-oriented, user-oriented building gains ground beyond "architecture with a big A" and how central "values and principles" were at the Eishin Campus. One went far beyond the application of a project language and worked with many other progressive design and construction methods. Neis addresses specific constructive aspects and Alexander's universal theory, as well as the goal of establishing design-build and self-building methods to create a livable, human and not least "beautiful architecture."

In order to clarify the principle of the Pattern Language, Christian Kühn, who had already visited the Eishin Campus in 2003, traces the theoretical prerequisites in his essay that Alexander formulated in the *Notes on the Synthesis of Form*. In this first basic theoretical text, Alexander deals with a methodly valid analysis of planning tasks, the aim of which is to subdivide an entire problem as precisely as possible into sub-problems that can be solved independently. In contrast, the Pattern Language is not linearly hierarchical, but built like a network in which a predictability of sub-problems is no longer assumed. Using the example of the 110-pattern "Project Language" for the Eishin Campus, Kühn sketches the design steps on the basis of which Alexander wanted to achieve a holistic architecture, as he later explained in his four-volume opus magnum *The Nature of Order*. Although Alexander's theory "seems to dissolve into the esoteric at this point," says Kühn, "it nonetheless remains stimulating when terms such as 'roughness,' 'echoes,' or 'thick boundaries' are discussed as geometrical properties." The question why Alexander's radical renewal of architecture is so strictly limited to the formal offerings of the past elliptically concludes with the charming counter-question as to which translation of *Pattern Language* Modernist architects such as Frank Lloyd Wright or Rudolph M. Schindler would have perhaps found.

In her text *"Urban Order and the Ambivalence of Patterns,"* architect and urban researcher Ida Pirstinger discusses Christopher Alexander's contribution to urban discourse, which is rooted in the British and American Design Methods movement of the 1960s. She contextualizes Alexander's highly acclaimed essay, *"A City is Not a Tree"* (1965) with writings of Jane Jacobs, Kevin Lynch and Jan Gehl that are critical of functionalism, expressing astonishment that *A Pattern Language*, despite its far-reaching reception, has hardly asserted itself in the planning practice of architecture and urbanism. She is ambivalent to the basic approach in *The Nature of Order,* in which Alexander tries to reconcile such fundamentally different things as nature, mathematics, scientific principles, and emotions with scientific means, especially since the binary juxtaposition of images and arguments suggests "that there would be a correct answer, as if everyone would see, think and feel the same." The pointed out connections, but also the differences between the methodological approaches of Alexander and the currents of New Urbanism, illustrate how much the attempts to rethink and re-build the city are branching out. "The deficits of the urban planning discipline are far from being resolved," Ida Pirstinger writes at the end of her article, but in the Age of the City it would be worthwhile to finally reflect the research, methods, and process development that have been carried out in recent decades on a broad basis. Christopher Alexander's legacy definitely belongs here.

In his essay written in 2007, architectural historian Norihito Nakatani addresses the question of why Christopher Alexander's work has hardly been received in Japan in the past two decades. He attributes the suppression of the Alexandrine theory—which resembles that in the West—to two factors: on one hand, the weakening of the ingeniously designing subject, who takes a back seat in an objectifiable planning process; on the other hand, the role of the unconscious, which Alexander attaches great importance to in the process of form-finding and which likewise opposes the autonomy of the individual who designs it. The pattern language, which empowers "everyone" to build a house, raises the question of who is meant by "everyone." The fact that it could be about something that exists independently of the conscious subject, and therefore eludes analytical access, probably contributed to the fact that it is rather difficult to follow Christopher Alexander on his development steps from *A Pattern Language* to the *Nature of Order*.

The last contribution features a Japanese architect of the younger generation—we meet Takaharu Tezuka at his studio on the periphery of Tokyo. Tezuka Architects gained international fame, especially with an unorthodox open-air kindergarten, reminding us in some aspects of Christopher Alexander's credo of holistic building. We want to know from Mr. Tezuka whether he is familiar with the Eishin Campus. Yes, he had visited it a long time ago and appreciated the village character of this complex very much. He had already come into contact with *A Pattern Language* as a student. Although he did not understand much of it until later, for him this book forms a kind of intuitive basis and grammar of his own language. "Timelessness" is also a key concept in his self-image as an architect. His idea of "timeless" architecture is primarily about the "luxury of inefficiency," experiencing something spontaneously and the direct experience of nature. *A Pattern Language* has provided the basis for these humanistic points of view, and one can build on this without imitating or copying. For his own work, Tezuka has coined the term *"Nostalgic Future,"* which includes the connection of longings with modern technology.

When we started researching for this book, it was clear to us that a wide field of uncertain edges would open up for us. What would we come across in dealing with a project realized 30 years ago, which, apart from a handful of journal articles, essentially only the planners themselves have written extensively about? Would our questions be the right ones?

In retrospect, the focus has shifted a bit and we are—through the trip to Tokyo and our own involvement with Christopher Alexander, through many discussions and through the contributions of our authors—immersed in an architect's world of thought that is elusive and has undergone numerous metamorphoses, whose thinking, planning, and building are always concerned with the "big picture." The fact that this attitude is met with skepticism and rejection is understandable. Our thesis that dealing with Alexander's theories, with his idea of a holistic, process-oriented and human architecture, is more worthwhile today than ever, that could indeed be a compelling alternative to conventional planning strategies, has been confirmed. With this book we hope to be able to make an impact with the genuine work of a great thinker—especially in view of the global challenges in architecture and urban planning—beyond the usual classifications into factions. In spite of all the justified relativism, is it perhaps worthwhile not to lose sight of the big picture?

"Look, my real goal is: I want the world to be more beautiful again." [3]

[3] "Von fließender Systematik und generativen Prozessen. Christopher Alexander im Gespräch mit Rem Koolhaas und Hans Ulrich Obrist," *ARCH+* 189, October 2008, 20–25.

View from the Kasumigaseki Building to the districts of Ginza and Shimbashi

Ernst Beneder
Tokyo, 1984

Arrival

Photographs by Ernst Beneder

1 ───────────────
Koji Taki, "Fragments and Noise," *Architectural Design* Vol. 5/6, 1988. Koji Taki, 1928–2011, photographer, publicist, critic, publisher, and one of the founders of the magazine *provoke* (1968). Taki commented on the Japanese architectural scene for decades as a photographer and essayist.

"For the record, two initial disclaimers: first, I have no desire to discuss Japanese architecture in terms of its 'unique Japanese-ness'; second, I am rather weary of the excesses of architectural discourse in general."
    Koji Taki introduces his 1988 article *"Fragments and Noise"*[1] with this clarification in order to discuss two paradigmatic structures from those years: Toyo Ito's house *Silver Hut* and Kazuo Shinohara's *Centennial Hall* of the Tokyo Institute of Technology. Both are representative of a Tokyo which increasingly considered itself as unique among the metropolitan regions. Taki then immediately addresses the global syncretism out of which the phenomenon of Tokyo and the attribution of being Japanese must be questioned as an excuse for being different. He is tired of constantly having an "anything goes," as it dominated the Tokyo architectural scene at the beginning of the 1980s, as sugarcoating it as avant-garde, on one hand, and as Japanese at the same time, or, on the other hand,—even worse—using these attributions interchangeably. In the instrumentalization of the "different," the hitherto unprecedented, the cliché, the prejudice, or a desire for exoticism and thereby everything, and be it to legitimize the largest meaningless bubble with loosely interpreted Far Eastern emptiness and alienness.
    At that time, pictures of strangely object-like houses that defied traditional architectural discourse reached the West. And this on the eve of postmodernism, where classical orders or pictorial nar-

ratives were striven for again elsewhere, not least to bring order into the cities that had become faceless.

Back to Japan: First there were the Metabolists from the 1960s, Kenzō Tange, Kiyonori Kikutake, the early Arata Isozaki. Their concepts and buildings were manifestos still indebted to a technical optimism, which culminated in Expo '70 in Osaka. But now, in the late 1970s and early 1980s, the small constructs of Tadao Ando, Toyo Ito and Kazuo Shinohara suddenly appeared. Enviously looked at, they were admired like a message from another world. Ando's *Row House in Sumiyoshi:* a minimalist cube. An atrium with only one opening to the street. Living, succinctly. Ito's *White U:* a horseshoe-shaped space. Narrow, unbounded in its retreating contour. Light falls through a narrow skylight band. Kazuo Shinohara's *Tanikawa House:* in the remote forest, a summerhouse for the poet Shuntarō Tanikawa. The ground in the incline of the slope. Freestanding wooden columns with slender struts under the simple gable roof. Shinohara calls the archaic-seeming structure a "zero-degree machine."[2]

It was Japan. It was avant-garde. And it was modernism. And yet rooted in the place and the region at the same time. Thus, when the rest of the world read Charles Jenck's *The Language of Postmodern Architecture* (1977), Kenneth Frampton gathered those aforementioned for his presentation on *Critical Regionalism* at the GA Gallery in Tokyo in 1984. And Frampton's insights into the topographic, social, and cultural pretexts spoke of the regional in a different form than was the case many times in Europe back then. Region in terms of the specific site. In the microcosm, as well as in the urban spatial horizon. Indebted to the geometric idea, like Raimund Abraham's *House for Euclid*. Yes, even a temporal head start, when an insight in one particular place is ahead of another elsewhere.[3]

The place, people agreed with Frampton at the GA Gallery, is determined by its topographic, social or historical particularity. In any case, not from a formal image imposed on him. Critical regionalism does not seek a role model or "preconception," but always poses a question in and about the present.

But it was not just the architects and urbanists who suddenly found interest in the still "unreachable" archipelago. At that time, the flight from Europe across the North Pole or across the Indian Ocean still took 26 hours and was almost unaffordable. The

---

[2] Cf. Kazuo Shinohara's essays: "When Naked Space Is Traversed," *JA* 76.02; "The Savage Machine as an Exercise," *JA* 79.03, and "Towards the 'Zero-Degree Machine,'" *Perspecta* 20.1983.

[3] Cf. Kenneth Frampton's article "The Isms of Contemporary Architecture," *AD* 52, 7/8–1982 (Modern Architecture and the Critical Present), London. On the occasion of the lecture in Tokyo in 1984, Kenneth Frampton used his essay "Towards a Critical Regionalism: Six Points for an Architecture of Resistance," edited by Hal Foster, *The Anti-Asthethic. Essays on Postmodern Culture*, Port Townsend, WA: Bay Press, 1983; as well as the article "Prospects for a Critical Regionalism," *Perspecta*. 20.1983, as a handout.

Far East actually was far. Roland Barthes titles the first chapter in his *L'Empire de signes*[4] "Là-bas"—"Faraway"—"Dort" ("There"), an essay of enchanting insight, view—yes, which "view?"— Barthes himself asks the question and describes how, as a viewer, he places himself in a different state of perception and becomes part of what he is looking at and thus of the event.

And they all first come late to Japan. Roland Barthes in 1966, to find himself "there" in a world which, as so many in the West, he had no idea of yet, as well as Claude Lévi-Strauss (five trips to Japan, 1979–1988), having arrived in Japan, thinking of himself as being on "the other face of the moon."[5] — From the outsider's view, there was no picture of what Ito and Shinohara intended to portray in their works. Not the "city" (often used in this context as a synonym for Tokyo) as a structurally recognizable place that can be communicated through this "imaging," but both objects tell about their conditions. Why the city is as it is. In its drawn tracks. In a spatial continuum that is not marked by built borders. But through relationships that unfold in interpenetrating spheres of activity. A flickering cosmos of small and very small magnetisms, which consolidate in a few places into virulent poles.

[4] 1970; English: *Empire of Signs*, trans. Richard Howard, New York: Hill & Wang, 1982.

[5] Claude Lévi-Strauss, *L'autre face de la lune: Écrits sur le Japon*, 2011; in English *The Other Face of the Moon*, trans. Jane Marie Todd, Cambridge, MA and London: The Belknap Press of Harvard University, 2013.

The Non-Depictable City

Everything built, no matter what scale, can be seen as a left-behind trace in the city and determines the ensuing and subsequent effect anew. In 1984, Kazuo Shinohara describes this progressive process of eruptive production, tracing, substitution, insertion and addition, and of change with the linguistic image of the "progressive anarchy," from which the city derives its vitality and the constant renewal of its essence. Shinohara shows us the Shibuya Station as an example, one of the main junctions of suburban and subway lines on the Yamanote Ring Railway.[6] A place which hardly any portrayal of Tokyo would have reported about at the time. One which, as a technical infrastructure, only makes accessible what should be the goal of the way and

[6] Kazuo Shinohara had repeatedly used the term "progressive anarchy" since 1984 in his lectures and writings, summarized in the essays "The Context of Pleasure" (in the section "A Metropolis, the Pleasure of No-Memory") and "A Program for the 'Fourth Space,'" both in JA 86.09.

the place to stay. But much more than anything else, the daily traveled distance becomes the city's collective place of identification.

Toyo Ito's *Silver Hut* and Shinohara's *Centennial Hall* are thus to be read as positions on the city in general and Tokyo in particular beyond the specific reason—the ephemeral, nomadically light entity that is indeterminate as a shape, as well as the monumental sculptural gesture of a deliberately abrupt "juxtaposition." Both objects tell more about the conditions of the city than about themselves, and are therefore in line with the many anonymous buildings, often on cramped plots of land, which embody the inherent necessity that shapes them in a similar way. Not least, the Japanese architects of post-war modernism had already found their forms in the topographical collisions and contradictions, and expressively articulated them, albeit with ostentatiously displayed technology and typologically-based structuring, as in Tange's *Shizuoka Press Center* (1967), Kurokawa's *Nakagin Capsule Tower* (1972) or Kikutake's *Pacific Hotel* (1966).

Silver Hut (Toyo Ito, 1984)

Tokyo Institute of Technology, Centennial Hall
(Kazuo Shinohara, 1984–1987)

Shinjuku, Ichibankan, "House No. 1"
(Minoru Takeyama, 1969)

For the most part, the concept for the solution is already concealed in the representation of the problem. Already freed from the reproach of arbitrary designing by the type of questioning (a task that often appears to be topographically insoluble), the sometimes bizarre-seeming structures attain something like a solitary autonomy and self-evidentness—as an answer in a dialogue that could not exist and be understood like that if the question (or the concrete construction task) had not been asked in this way (or especially in this place). Giving space in Tokyo always means first having the chance to recognize one. It is immanent in Shinohara and Ito that they recognize a "problematique"—as Taki writes—in the task that was to be solved and, answered concretely, then withstood a universal examination.

Against the background of Tokyo's uniqueness described by the feature pages in the early 1980s, the "Japanese-ness" mentioned at the beginning is to be viewed critically. After all, the discussion of Tokyo's urban space is primarily about a concrete analysis of the situation, which at first glance does not refer back to the Japanese building tradition. Rather, the subject is an in-between, a literal reciprocal of the figurative. Consequently, a spatial frame of mind that is difficult to depict. In 1984, only a few people outside Japan had knowledge or a pictorial imagination of this conditioning, as it applied, for instance, to Paris and London with their landmarks, or New York with its skyline. This place (i.e., Tokyo) was not sought. Not as a travel destination or desired place of residence. And one believed to be able to pass by it on the way to the historical buildings in Kyōto.

Nakagin Capsule Tower
(Kisho Kurokawa, 1972)

7
Lévi-Strauss, from the "Interview with Junzo Kawada" (1993), *The Other Face of the Moon*, trans. Jane Marie Todd, Cambridge, MA and London: The Belknap Press of Harvard University, 2013, 146.

Claude Lévi-Strauss, for example, reports that he had been warned against the ugliness of Tokyo: *"'Above all, don't be daunted by Tokyo. Tokyo is an ugly city.' Well, I did not have that impression at all in modern Tokyo, because I found myself liberated from something that I did not suspect was so constrictive in our civilizations, namely, streets! Streets with houses all stuck together, while the buildings in Tokyo are put up with much more freedom, so to speak, and constantly leave an impression of diversity."*[7]

Despite the many contradictions, Tokyo leaves behind the impression of a complex whole in which a quality of life so unexpected is hidden. Not just in parks or gardens. Not just in the zones designed for it. However, in many unanticipated, inconspicuous and unintended situations. Transitorily understood space presents a challenge per se. First of all, to accept it. Then to cope with it. To find your way around, to move. Not understood as a goal and sought, it suddenly becomes the place of lingering. And grants the freedom described by Lévi-Strauss. From a Western point of view, Japanese architecture has often been denied the sense of space. The opposite seems to be the case, since the mere suggestion of unfolding this for the one approaching suffices.

One would like to add, on occasion. Where space is not marked by staking boundaries it is determined by pervasive—and simultaneous—presences. It also contains space for sharing, one of use rather than appropriation, as Kazunari Sakamoto describes in his 1981 essay *"Transcending the Residence as an Object of Ownership."*[8]

[8] First published in 1981 in *Shin Kenchiku,* later in *House: Poetics of the Ordinary*, Tokyo: Toto Publishers, 2001; cf. also "From Architecture as an Object to Space as an Environment," *JA* 86.11.

The Unintentional City

Tokyo fascinates people with its multi-layered and ambiguous scale. The supply works from the early hours on and until late at night. Numerous small shops and small retailers line the way. This smallness is also found in the fluid transition between the stalls, their closed and open areas and the presented goods. These open borders also show up between the mini-houses. Space still "left open" and indefinite exists at the thresholds. To recognize this, however, the shifted view, the other disposition of perception, the "shock of meaning," as Roland Barthes describes it, is already required. And he makes clear that the talk is of everyday life, not of art, folklore or civilization per se.[9]

[9] Barthes, *Empire of Signs*, 4.

The heterogeneous, the loud ("random noise," Shinohara), the askew ("visual cacophony," Itsuko Hasegawa) of the built fabric—measured against the whole—suddenly appears secondary, the bulky and the ugly not particularly disturbing. The consensus lies in the social code, in the disposition to the integration into the common, as, for example, the labyrinthine network of public transport lines. Apart from the city highways and a few thoroughfares, the motorized individual traffic seems secondary and withdrawn. Miniature-like, only for the occasion anyhow. The major centers are thereby shaped by the infrastructure of public transport and its associated services. The knots along the Yamanote Line—most notably the stations Shibuya, Shinjuku, Shinagawa, as well as Ueno, Akihabara or Shimbashi. Time and again, it is the unique topography that compels us to unrepeatable constellations and unique spatial ingenuity, and thus leads to concrete memory.

The example of Shibuya Station: Situated in a valley, the suburban, underground and main lines come along at different levels and stack their platforms, halls and tracks, piled up in a construct more reminiscent of Piranesi's *Carceri* than a technical traffic structure in the modern sense. The Ginza Line finds its way between two skyscrapers on a high bridge, spans over the bus station and flows into the upper floors of the station complex. On another level, incoming buses are turned on a turntable to be able to drive out again. The scene is reminiscent of Fritz Lang's urban visions in his film *Metropolis*. However, lying in the provisional nature of the layers and surfaces overlying the hard core of the station is a latent cheerfulness, a character of simple, never quite finished suburban train stations and branch lines. The threatening totalitarianism, as depicted in Fritz Lang's vision, remains distant.

Shibuya Station, with the Tōyoko Line in the foreground

Shibuya, Hachiko Square, looking into the city

Shibuya, Hachiko Square, looking out of the city

Shimbashi Station, behind it Kenzō Tange's Shizuoka Press Center

Shibuya, Meiji-Dori with the Ginza Line

Ginza Line, entrance into Shibuya Station

Tokyo has undergone an enormous transformation process since 1984. At that time, the city with its technical structures was an analogue apparatus with the corresponding soundscape and light backdrop. Years before the mobile phone. Lettering only in Japanese characters. No screens in public space. Platform conductors with clattering ticket punchers. Shrill pachinko gambling halls next to them. Small kitchens and stalls. The unceasing welcome call "Irasshai mase!" The direct and shortest way is almost never to be perceived easily. Stairs that frequently lead up and down. Always an unexpected entrance. In the smallest and most cramped niche, nevertheless useful, obvious, continuing. In addition to that, the perceptible surfaces are constantly changing, pushing themselves into the foreground with the offered wares and ads shaped by the Japanese kanji characters. The background, or rather the many levels of physical background, always remain mere intimations in these permeable layers, themselves becoming "signs" that carry on in the spatial continuum.

Cherry blossom, Ueno Park

Side street in Nakano

Tokyo was described back then as the city of the late 20th century, as one that anticipated the structure of post-industrial society and accommodated the vision of a city of the information society. Not in adaptation to the European city of the 19th century. But also not designed according to that of the classical modern age. The density of services and the "cityscape" freed from emblems and landmarks seemed to satisfy this lookout. Often, the impression of the city arises precisely where it was not intended as such, but as something that was conceived as access into it.

[10]
Walter Benjamin, *Gesammelte Schriften III*, Frankfurt: Suhrkamp Verlag, 1972–1989, 368; cf. also Benjamin, *Über Städte und Architekturen*, Detlev Schöttker, ed., Berlin: DOM publishers, 2017; and Benjamin, *Das Passagenwerk*, Frankfurt: Suhrkamp Verlag, 1982

[11]
Toyo Ito, "Exhibition Project for the Pao as a Dwelling of Tokyo's Nomad Woman" (1985) is illustrated in numerous monographs; first published in *JA* 85.12 and *Shin Kenchiku* 85.12.

For Walter Benjamin, the passage was already the paradigm of such a transitory space and the status of transit, that of the flâneur, of the highest willingness to perceive and participate. For Benjamin, it was about feeling spaces. Therefore, it's not about seeing, but about "sensing through structures."[10] The extended scope of action leads to constantly penetrating new, but similarly open spaces. There, in the open and indefinite, "space" is "brought along" as a personal disposition. Relieved of the bonds and obligations in the state of "correspondence," in the constant "transfer." It was Toyo Ito who exemplarily illustrated the nomadic way of life aptly with his installation *Dwelling of Tokyo's Nomad Woman* (1985). In this image, consumerism is limited to the—albeit luxurious—mobile consumer goods and already leaves the heaviness of the sedentary behind.[11]

Liberation from Meaning. Language as an Operative Comparison

[12]
As of 1966, Roland Barthes undertook three journeys to Japan in rapid succession. Cf. *Empire of Signs*, 99 and 80.

[13]
Cf. Atsushi Miagawa, "In the Blank of the Theory of Maniera," *JA* 76.03; Toyo Ito, "Dismantling the Meaning Space," *JA* 77.12, as well as monographic reviews, e.g., *JA* 87.07 or *SD* 86.02; Hiromi Fujii, "Deconstruction through Differentiation – Metamorphology, Desemiotization, Traces and Deconstruction," *Kenchiku Bunka,* July 1985, resp., *JA* 95.09.

The difficulty of depicting the multilayered character of the city makes the viewers tell about their events, using the language itself as an image-drawing medium and at the same time drawing upon the language as a metaphor of what is being told about it.

In the descriptions of Japanese architecture there is often talk of a grammar to be felt out. Sometimes this is limited to visual perception, that is, to recognizing graphic patterns of predominantly small-scale, but recurring particles. Once in Japan, Roland Barthes finds "ideographic characters" and himself in a "graphic mode of existing."[12] The architects and authors look for syntactic rules and get lost in far-fetched thoughts, as well as in the serious quest for helpful structures to present their design methodology. Arata Isozaki talks about "maniera," Toyo Ito about "morpheme." And Hiromi Fujii describes it as geometric "disemiotization (sic!),"[13] just to name a few. Always in the hypothesis that such a set of rules can be found in the apparently fluid, in the chaotic, unretainable. And if such a set is at the root of it, then it is hidden (Yoshinobu Ashihara, 1986), but yet omnipresent, all-encompassing, translatable, thus also "learnable" and applicable. At least there is an understanding, a social code, an attitude of tolerance and a basic trust in the common use of the city. What is amazing for a city of this size is the absence of the enemy, the perceptible defense, the barriers, the gates.

Ookayama, Oimachi Line, view from the main entrance of the Tokyo Institute of Technology

The existence of rules first allows the possibility to defy them and to reflect about this on the meta-level of difference. Thus, a "grammar" after all! One that, per se, does not give meaning to a sentence but, in the confinement of the message, gives it poetic potential regardless of its comprehensibility. And thus conveys the impression of a language. Does it now apply to decipher a language from the given, or to impose a language on the chaotic?

For Koji Taki, language is essential to define architecture. However, the excessive discourse of explaining architecture as a kind of language leads to superficial and ambiguous terms—just "designations" and assignments of meaning. Brought into play—and often missing—as a design methodical approach, his "problematique" primarily develops the possibilities of architecture as something open ("oeuvres ouvertes") in the sense of being regarded as something set up initially free of meaning—with culture as the "prétexte," against the

WHAT WE UNDERSTAND.

DOES NOT SIMPLY STAND RIGID.

IT MOVES ITSELF, US.

[14] Taki, "Fragments and Noise."

[15] Cf. Gilles Deleuze and Félix Guattari, *L'Anti-Œdipe,* Paris: Les Éditions du Minuit, 1972; English, *Anti-Oedipus: Capitalism and Schizophrenia,* trans. Robert Hurley, Mark Seem, and Helen R. Lane, Minneapolis: University of Minnesota Press, 1983; Deleuze and Guattari, *Kafka. Pour une littérature mineure,* Paris: Les Éditions du Minuit, 1975; English, *Kafka: Toward a Minor Literature,* trans. Dana Polan, Minneapolis: University of Minnesota Press, 1986

[16] Quoted in *Japanische Architektur, Geschichte und Gegenwart,* Manfred Speidel, ed., Dusseldorf: Hatje, 1983, originally published in *JA* 79.04 ("In Search of the House Form").

background of which a building substantiates this pretext as a "texte," and would thus give it meaning in an "écriture" determined by this process.[14]

It is noticeable that Taki and many other authors in Japan adopt their central concepts from the French. The reception of structuralism and the linguistic works of Roland Barthes, such as *Le degré zéro de l'écriture* or *Le plaisir du texte,* does not lie far back and is soon reflected in the positions of the Japanese avant-garde. Again and again, the question of the semantic content and the one giving the meaning is posed. The idea of the "degré zéro," with which Barthes discusses the "mythology of literary expression," comes in very handy in this discourse. Buildings initially designed free of meaning are often described as "machines." Not in the sense of the steamship aesthetics of modernity. Rather, it uses Gilles Deleuze's metaphor, which ascribes a text the mechanism of being able to produce meaning. *"Textes"* after all.[15] But texts of what content? How much is the city, as a "text," one of its stories? About events? Or does it merely describe everyday life?

Kazunari Sakamoto's monograph, in which he summarizes his houses that hardly stand out from the urban fabric, is entitled *House: Poetics in the Ordinary.* Already in 1979 he describes his approximation to the living environment of Tokyo:

"I cannot remember exactly, but the house I was looking for had a simple, house-like shape. Simple, but well-kept—not crude—it stood in a corner of the city and left no doubt about its presence. Without being conspicuous, it did not disappear between the surrounding houses. Although its neighbors stood there very self-confidently, this house was quiet; it did not want to say anything [...]. As an image, it was a fantastic contrast to its surroundings; but one cannot call it anything but a house [...], perhaps precisely the simplicity makes a description so difficult."[16]

The narrative introduces the temporal sequence as a further dimension to the consideration, as one of relationships and events. These require communication and that the viewer also engages with the narrator, which presupposes an agreement with the city itself. Acceptance of contemporary everyday life assumes leaving behind the expectations shaped by images of historical Japanese architecture. This claim is not new. Bruno Taut, like Frank Lloyd Wright, was disappointed about the loss of traditional Japanese way of building. Taut, who "simply could not comprehend this loud, hideous hodgepodge"

[17] Bruno Taut, *Houses and People of Japan*, trans. Estille Balk, Tokyo: The Sanseido Co. Ltd., 1937, 295.

in Tokyo, had come to Japan in 1933 to live in exile—and stayed. His writings testify to the admiration of Japanese culture, the highest perfection of which he found in the Katsura Villa in Kyōto, which he declared as "world architecture."[17]

Monorail, next to Haneda International Airport

Passageway, Ueno Station

Yamanote Line near Ueno, Ameyoko

View from the Sunshine 60 Building, Ikebukuro

Fujigaoka Station forecourt, Den-en Toshi Line

Side street in Nakano

Wright, who had built the Imperial Hotel in Tokyo in 1923, was also an admirer of Japan and in 1936 lamented the loss of civilization in Tokyo as he found it: "Japan has no civilization now. She threw hers away to borrow one …"[18]

[18] Wright in a letter to Aisaku Hayashi, dated July 6, 1936; Frank Lloyd Wright, *Letters to Architects*, Fresno: The Press at California State University, Frank Lloyd Wright Memorial Foundation, 1984.

Since then, Tokyo had been destroyed and rebuilt several times, which obviously did not detract from its hidden inherent uniqueness, as later effusive reports and analyses show. An amazement that Wim Wenders still uses in 1985 as part of his cinematic narrative about the Japanese filmmaker Yasujiro Ozu. The title, *Tokyo-Ga*, in itself, is only understandable in the Japanese language, roughly: "Tokyo, that." In the flash-

Meguro Station, Yamanote Line

back to Ozu's *Tokyo Monogatari* (*The Tokyo Story,* 1953), he manages to create continuity for a city completely different in its visual appearance, namely the one from the 1950s. The only thing entirely different is the image of the city district still completely built of simple wooden houses, as the background of the "Japanese-ness," which does not tell a story about the scenery, but about the complex network of relationships of its protagonists.

In Wim Wenders' film (shot in 1983), Tokyo was still flat, with the exception of the Shinjuku district, with about a dozen skyscrapers and the distant, freestanding Ikebukuro skyscraper on the horizon. Together with the *Tokyo Tower* located near the city center, navigation in the horizonless city was thus possible. Like a compass, Ikebukuro showed the northern loop of the Yamanote Line, the skyline of Shinjuku the western one. In the center, the oft-discussed emptiness of the Imperial Palace—inaccessible, yet giving scale and a topographic hold to a constantly circulating urban society.

At the end of the 1980s—Japan suddenly finds itself in the spotlight of economic and cultural interest—the foreignness, perceived as congenial and never threatening, becomes the stereotype of chic "Japanese-ness" in design and fashion. The incomprehensible and the unattainable now fascinate a wider audience, even if the city itself is increasingly approaching the West and its standards. In the film *Lost in Translation* (Sofia Coppola, 2003), the protagonists are—two decades after 1984—still facing an "untranslatable" Tokyo, even though the setting described is one of contemporary high technology. The unknowable is already deprived of its meaningful background and is ultimately not communicated in the film.

Intermediate Space: Openness and Indeterminacy

The awareness of space in the traditional Japanese house, as well as coping with the density of contemporary cities, are based on the demand for presence and the acceptance of its transitory space, but by no means on its pictorially memorable marking. Space is often the personal projection as a response to its mere suggestion. The difficult-to-translate concept of *Ma*, the Japanese ideogram for space in the broadest sense as a spatial and temporal interval, is always to be read anew. It was just Arata Isozaki, one of the Metabolists of the 1960s and later the leading protagonist of postmodernism, who brought the news of enigmatic Japan into the avant-garde discourse in the West with his spectacular and prominently placed exhibition *Ma – Space-Time* in Japan. The exhibition was first shown in 1979 at the Cooper Hewitt Museum in New York and then at the Centre Pompidou in Paris, as well as in Houston, Chicago, Stockholm and Helsinki.

Advertising structures in Nishi-Shinjuku

Considered by the West as a found key to grasping "the Japanese," the character *Ma* is quickly read in a simplistic—and engrossing—way. Pointing it out as unfathomable and untranslatable, even the avant-garde in Tokyo tenaciously insists on its "uniqueness," its "Japanese-ness," the unique position of Tokyo, which this character alone was to prove.

As a character it is a simple diagram: speaking of the in-between. Of the interval. Light falls through the open door. Right now, at this moment. Here. In the figurative sense it may mean a "local and temporal spell," as "luck" and "chance" it speaks of the relationship potential that offers an open space to the viewer. To understand this, a look at the zoning in the Japanese house is helpful. First of all, the topography: access, vestibule, surface, tatami mats, sliding walls. The wide-spreading roof. Space, delimited and determined at the same time. The traditional Japanese house may be an obvious comparative example of a city structure that first finds its meaning in its use and otherwise escapes any definition. A city of intervals. But in its vagueness, Tokyo's reality also conveys that it leaves space open for something else. Interstices, in which both tolerance and experiment find their place.

Tsukuba Center Building
(Arata Isozaki, 1983)

House in Yokohama (Kazuo Shinohara, 1984)

Yoyogi Olympic Stadium
(Kenzō Tange, 1964)

Midorigaoka, apartment building in a side street

Like Isozaki's *Tsukuba Center Building* (1983) with an inverse replica of Michelangelo's Piazza at the Capitol in Rome. Or Itsuko Hasegawa's *Shonandai Bunka Center* (1991): serially arranged, pyramid-shaped kiosks support an auditorium enveloped in a globe. Or Toyo Ito's *Restaurant Nomad* (1986): cloud-like, drifting surfaces of expanded metal. Temporary space reserved for a temporary stay. At the peripheral centers there are theme parks such as a miniature Venice in Jiyūgaoka or love hotels with motifs playing between science fiction and fantasy. Much of it is quickly raised and remains short-lived, not only the consumer architecture, but also main works of Ito, Hasegawa, even Tange and Shinohara. Tange's City Hall, dating back to 1957, already gave way to Rafael Viñoly's Tokyo International Forum in 1996. Even Shinohara's own house, the *House in Yokohama* (completed in 1984) is already a thing of the past.

Industrial plants in Kawasaki

City highway over the course of a river near Nihombashi

A look at Tokyo in 1984 gives a snapshot of a constant, progressing process. A shimmering game of events. It seems as if the virulence, the lightness associated with it, could be lost in an increasingly finished and immovably-built Tokyo. Distinctive structures, even those like Shibuya Station, disappear nearly unnoticed. Others fall into the shadows of sprawling high-rise clusters. Smooth, clear and additive. Nothing hidden lures. Without narratives, the city becomes more incomprehensible. In the disappointment of not being able to surmise something hidden, silent to the beholder.

The Tokyo of 1984 is also the Tokyo of Toyo Ito and Kazuo Shinohara. But it was these two who discovered another one: the cosmos of countless stations, niches and transitions, the "juxtapositions" and "correspondences," a secret space in the crowd.

Christopher Alexander built the Eishin Campus on the northwestern outskirts of Tokyo from 1982 to 1987.

Marunouchi, forecourt in front of the Imperial Palace

Library tract in the original College Building

Walter Ruprechter
On the Cultural Ambiguity of the Eishin Campus

First you have to find the Eishin Campus of Higashino High School in Greater Tokyo. Although the train stations near it are relatively good and easily accessible, the final approach must be by bus. This then chugs half an hour through completely indefinable terrain with consistently low development, which alternates between residential, commercial and agricultural use, until you get to the exit point at a small Christian chapel. There you stand on the street and look around for the famous complex of buildings that will soon catch your eye. A view of a hill occasionally opens up between a narrow tangle of houses, revealing strangely tall buildings that appear like a Fata Morgana. This impression is reinforced when you notice that the closer you think you are, the farther away the mirage is. Of course, there is no direct access to the object; after all, we are moving on Japanese ground.

This Fata Morgana-like quality remains, even when you have finally infiltrated the Campus and look onto the school grounds from the height of the somewhat distant cafeteria. A peculiar ensemble of larger and smaller buildings, paths, squares, bridges and patches of water and meadow stretches before you like the vision of an ideal *community,* as the builder of this Campus, Christopher Alexander, might have had when he gazed upon the tea fields that had previously extended out here from the very same heights. Even today's visitor shares this vision, the reason for which may lie in an oscillation that keeps the eye of the beholder incessantly busy and lets him/her jump between different codings of the seen—an oscillation, as Alexander himself has described in his theory of overlapping.

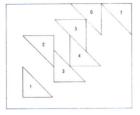

Analysis of a work of art by Simon Nicholson, from Alexander: "A City is Not a Tree," *Architectural Forum*, 2.1965, vol. 122, 62

1 ——————————————
Christopher Alexander, "A City is Not a Tree," 21. Available at http://www.en.btu.edu.tw/wp-content/uploads/2011/12/06-Alexander-A-city-is-not-a-tree.pdf

In his 1965 essay *"A City is Not a Tree,"* Alexander explains the theory of overlapping using the example of a painting by the artist Simon Nicholson. The painting shows seven right-angled triangles set in a diagonal arrangement from bottom left to top right. Three triangles open to the right face four open to the left, forming counter elements turned 180°. This gives rise to the possibility that, together with differentiated shadowing of the triangular surfaces, they converge in the eye of the beholder to form various figurations. Alexander writes that the respective elements (triangles) work together, creating larger figurative units: rectangles, parallelograms, enclosures, inclusions, directional figures, etc. What makes it special is that all these figures overlap in one element (triangle) and these overlaps create the structure of this painting.

"The painting is significant, not so much because it has overlap in it (many paintings have overlap in them), but rather because this painting has nothing else in it except overlap. It is only the fact of the overlap, and the resulting multiplicity of aspects which the forms present, that makes the painting fascinating. It seems almost as though the painter had made an explicit attempt, as I have done, to single out overlap as a vital generator of structure."[1]

The effect of this painting, therefore, is an oscillation between different figurations, a permanent change of shapes in the eye of the beholder. The image keeps the eye incessantly busy by fitting the triangle elements into ever-changing units.

At the end of the essay, Alexander endeavors to clarify his actual theme, the structure of natural cities as opposed to so-called drawing-board cities. The contrast between the two urban structures consists in the fact that in natural cities, user functions overlap at certain elements of the city's set, thus creating urban structure, while the structure of artificial cities is formed of separate functions. As an example of the former, he describes a situation at a crossroads with a traffic light, where a drugstore with a newspaper rack is also located. When the traffic light turns red, pedestrians must wait. Their eyes then fall on the newspapers displayed on the newsrack. Some read the headlines, others buy the newspaper, money changes owners. Elements of the set thus start to interact:

"This effect makes the newsrack and the traffic light interactive; the newsrack, the newspapers on it, the money going from people's pockets to the dime slot, the people who stop at the light and read papers, the traffic light, the electric impulses which make

the lights change, and the sidewalk which the people stand on form a system—they all work together." [2]

In each element, actions of city users overlap, forming superordinate patterns of action, thus creating the structure of a natural city in which the areas of life are not artificially separated, but interact and overlap in a variety of ways. They form a structure that Alexander calls a "semilattice" and that is distinguished from the simpler tree structure in that it contains infinitely more possible combinations of the elements. The structure of a natural city consists of very complex interaction patterns, but they are bound to a set of manageable elements.

The question now is to what extent this semilattice structure has been applied to the Eishin Campus. Ultimately, it is also about creating an interaction space that should correspond to an ideal interaction of various factors.

In the mentioned essay, Christopher Alexander stressed that it is difficult for the human mind to grasp the complexity of a semilattice structure because of its natural growth. The mind tends to resolve the simultaneity of events generated by a semilattice structure into simple linearity and map it in a tree structure. "Semilattice" is thus initially understood as an analysis category suitable for conceiving naturally grown structures. The creation of "communities" that would correspond to the complexity of urban growth would therefore not be possible by means of rational planning, since the human mind would be overwhelmed in dealing with the necessary complexity and ambiguity of events. (Whether high performance computers are capable of doing this is not discussed in this essay).

As an architect of communities, Alexander now appears to have carved out his own approach to such complexity apart from abstractly rational planning with his invention of the Pattern Language, which implicates an involvement of all potential users in the process of planning the facility to be built.

In the case of the Eishin Campus, he described this process in detail in his book, *The Battle for the Life and Beauty of the Earth,* a retrospective account of the conflict-laden history of the project. Unlike many architects, Alexander begins his project with an in-depth questioning of everyone involved about ideas, desires, and dreams with respect to the construction project, in this case a campus for a high school with an attached college. Not only teachers and students, but

[2] Ibid. 2.

also Campus employees should express their opinions on the functioning and appearance of the facilities. These opinions are conveyed and evaluated by Alexander's team in months of discussions and, as a collective ideal, form the basis for the development of a pattern language of over one hundred patterns for the Eishin Campus. The next step for the project team entails going to the site of the development and projecting those visions onto the site. Imaginary structures are thereby defined through the distribution of the buildings, paths and squares, which are then marked and staked out with the help of real flags on the grounds. Only then does the architect begin to work with sketches on paper and, in further teamwork, form models for the spatial structure and design the appearance of the building in detail. The architect's plan, therefore, is merely the attempt to fixate a collective vision in which the ideas and desires of the users flow together with the experience and knowledge of the project team, and are trimmed to their feasibility. Plans are only means to steer a collective process from the imaginary to the real, but in no way proof of the genius of an individual who defies all circumstances in a self-actualization process. The process remains open for modifications during the entire construction period and, in its openness, is to anticipate the complexity of the facility users' real life.

In addition to these general principles of an alternative planning process, Alexander's method of participation also contains interesting aspects from a cultural scientific point of view, since the Eishin Campus is a project realized by an Austrian-American architectural visionary, Christopher Alexander, with a Japanese school visionary, Hisae Hosoi, in his country, Japan. Although the intercultural factors of this project are blinded out by Alexander himself in favor of a Manichean *two-world system*, the questions of the cultural conditionality of his method are, of course, self-evident. This begins with very simple facts: What stands behind a school building, naturally, is an educational system that is certainly developed differently in cultures as distant as the American and the Japanese, although Japanese society has been influenced the most by American society since the Second World War and, for instance, also adopted the college system.

    Moreover, it has to be taken into account that Japanese spatial design also works in the public domain according to other principles, not only in terms of materials or standards, but also in regard to exterior and interior, the function of streets, squares and gardens, the symbolism of building elements such as columns or roof forms, but also water courses, stones or bridges and, ultimately, the structure of the public sphere as such. All of this is not specifically mentioned in the *Battle,* and the question of how far Alexander and his American team dealt with Japanese culture at all cannot be found in the book. Alexander's assertion that the whole world is pervaded by an irreconcilable dual system of the good pursuit of beauty ("System A"), on the one hand, and the evil pursuit of profit ("System B"), on the other hand, and all cultural differences would be marginalized in the process is, in spite of its questionable simplification, not necessarily an indication of cultural ignorance, because its method of participation is able to absorb cultural differences in the construction process in a very different way and to inscribe them in the buildings themselves.

Since the principle of participation is to derive the structure and layout of the facility from the concrete suggestions of the users, it is clear that features of their culture also emerge. Thus, if tatami mats are required in certain spaces, seat cushions instead of chairs, translucent sliding elements *(shōji)* running parallel to the windows, if it is suggested that the shoes are to be taken off in the classrooms, as is stated in the pattern language for the Eishin Campus, then obvious features of Japanese culture are automatically incorporated into the project. The inscribing can also be done more subtly, for example, through the suggestion:

"The way from the gate to the building should not be straight but winding." And further: *"This entrance way should have some trees alongside, especially trees with big leaves which fall in autumn, change colors. Wants to see the change of seasons in these trees."*[3]

In the question of materials and in details of the building design, there are also guidelines from the pattern language which enrich the project with Japanese cultural elements. However, at first sight it is not easy to see what the Japanese character of the Campus would be, as an experiment with Japanese students showed. Their first impression of the Campus in photos was consistently that—apart from the bridge over the pond—it concerned a Western facility. Only a closer examination of details reveals Japanese elements therein, such as the *teri-mukuri* line of Japanese temple architecture over the portal of the Judo Hall, small garden arrangements with low entrance gates, or some ornaments on the moldings, which extend over several buildings. The heavy, hanging beams of the sports hall are reminiscent of ancient temple constructions in Nara (*Tōdai-ji*) or

Christopher Alexander et al., *The Battle for the Life and Beauty of the Earth. A Struggle Between Two World-Systems* (Center for Environmental Structure, Book 16), New York: Oxford University Press, 2012, 129.

3 ———

Nara, Tōdai-ji Shrine

Gymnasium

Judo Hall, side entrance

of townhouses in Takayama (*Kusakabe*). In order to be able to also notice "turned and bent axes" (Manfred Speidel) in the complex, a more specialized knowledge about Japanese architecture is already required. And are there not allusions to terms as well? The technique of *kura shikkui* (black plaster) applied to the façade of the sports hall points (me) tonally to the western Japanese town of Kurashiki, whose *kura* (= storehouse) architecture is alluded to in the adjacent classroom front.

What is rumored in relation to Bruno Taut's house on the Bosporus, namely that the builder himself regarded it as a/his Japanese house, while Japanese visitors considered it a Western one, may also apply here. The cultural coding, therefore, is probably also associated with the apperception, which, in turn, is culturally coded itself.

Alexander, whom his Japanese admirers call simply Alex, certainly struck a chord with the Japanese with his *Pattern Language*. The collective and unconscious approach, capable of undermining the rationality of an individual's planning, not only earned him the attention of architects, but also secured him an important place in the critique of rationalism by Kōjin Karatani, the most important contemporary Japanese philosopher. In his book *Architecture as Metaphor,* he praises Alexander's essay *"A City is Not a Tree"* as an example of what a deconstruction of Western planning rationality can look like without abandoning the "will to architecture." And although this "will to architecture" has never existed in Japan, Alexander's concept of "natural" systems is closer to Japanese architects' ideas of the creative process.

Kyōto, Katsura Villa

Perhaps the best way to prove this is with Arata Isozaki, who wrote a great deal about the different concepts of design in the West and in Japan. Interesting in this regard is his book *Katsura Villa: The Ambiguity of Its Space,* in which he criticizes Bruno Taut for insinuating that the builder of the Katsura Rikyū Imperial Villa in Kyōto, Kobori Enshū, has a perception of an architectural genius, who, in an individual Herculean task, would have cleansed Japanese culture of Chinese influence and restored it in the pure Japanese spirit in a complex. Isozaki says that this is an inappropriate idea for the 17th century in Japan, since Enshū's work is not to be comprehended in individualistic categories. The real people responsible for the design and construction of the complex were rather the anonymous carpenters and horticulturists proceeding according to the rules of traditional craftsmanship, while Enshū held a position that assured his *"supervision of the Katsura project, in that he must have determined, or approved, the concept and direction of the design."* Above all, he was responsible for the aesthetic coordination of the construction process, which is why the term *Enshū-konomi* has become established. *Konomi* is a word for taste or style, so *Enshū-konomi* means something like Enshū-taste or Enshū-style, which indeed characterizes the aesthetic of the whole of the complex, but is not the result of any individualistic concept. The proper name Enshū does not stand for authorship in the Western sense, but for a system or a method:

> *"It is perfectly correct to say that Enshū was not the author of Katsura Villa. But it is also correct to say that the* konomi—*the 'system' and methods that may be discerned—was indeed Enshū's. This is to claim, in terms of a certain Japanese logic, that the design method that produced Katsura Villa is ultimately attributable to Enshū. Therefore it is possible to call it 'Enshū's design'. But according to the Western view, Enshū did* not *design the architecture and the garden, so Enshū was not the designer. Here there is indeed a cultural gap."*[4]

Arata Isozaki, *Katsura: Imperial Villa*, London: Phaidon Press, 2005, 292, 295.

4 ──────────

Would it be possible to see the Eishin Campus as an attempt to close this *"cultural gap?"* And could one not also speak analogously of Alexander-konomi? The withdrawal of his individual claim to the coordination of a collective design achievement, as building according to the pattern language entails, has come against a traditional notion of construction in Japan and has found correspondingly broad resonance. The concept of *konomi* also consists of descriptive instructions on how a complex, various spaces, squares and paths, individual details, etc., are to be designed or used, and is therefore likewise formulated in a type of pattern language. In the case of the tea house, for example, it is stated (according to Isozaki) that:

> *"(1) the room should be a little larger than four tatami mats ... (2) guest should be seated only to the right of the host; (3) there should be an additional room called the kusari-no-ma next to the main tearoom ... (4) there are to be eight windows; (5) the proportion of a shōji grid should be one by two; (6) a picture should be placed at the focal point of the space."*

This is not unlike the pattern language of the Eishin Campus, where it says: *"All homebase classrooms will have big windows facing south. If possible, the glare from these windows may be modified by the existence of a gallery, about 1 meter away from the window. Sliding screens, translucent, run parallel to window. [...]"*

Such descriptions thus form the basis for the design of the structures and limit the individual design claim to the formal implementation of such patterns. Perhaps Buffon's dictum applies to Alexander-konomi, according to which the style is the human being himself/herself, which implies that his/her individuality is expressed anyhow in his/her actions, without him/her having to elevate it to an axiom. This form of individuality also does not produce any unambiguities, but, as Isozaki attests for Kobori Enshū, rather an *"ambiguity of its space."*

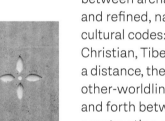

The visual appearance of the Eishin Campus and its buildings thus remains enigmatically ambivalent. In its shapes and atmospheres it oscillates between alien and familiar, sacral auratic and secular, between archaic and modern, timeless and historical, between rough and refined, natural and stage-like. It alternates between different cultural codes: traditional and modernist Japanese, Northern European Christian, Tibetan Buddhist and not least American Alexandrian. From a distance, the Campus even oscillates between real and virtual. In its other-worldliness it shows itself to the observer who is swinging back and forth between cultures as a phenomenon in-between visionary construction and built vision.

Hisae Hosoi at Café Almond, Tokyo, April 2017

Hisae Hosoi
"Sweet Home in My Heart"

An ambiguous image before meeting with Chris

Photography: Mao Matsuda

The Board of Directors of Eishin School decided on the Eishin Project in December, 1980. The school was selling its site in Musashino City, Tokyo, in order to get a bigger plot of land near Tokyo for a new Campus. Its main structure was to be a complex of low-rise wooden facilities with a wooden gym, Judo Hall and only one heavy steel structured Great Hall ...

The two principles to build our new Campus were a big enough site and a low-rise wooden structure. I had already said "good bye" to modern architecture then, because of having experienced deep disappointment in a forest of topic-making modern school buildings. They were nicely designed by modern architects and their system of function for schools matched to their beautiful designs quite well. How-ever, the spaces I saw in them were inorganic and cold. They did not have any space of sweet memory. When I visited Oak Park in Chicago, Illinois in the US, several old-fashioned residences designed by Frank Lloyd Wright attracted me a lot with their spaces of sweet memory. Since then, I had dreamt of having such spaces everywhere on our new Campus.

When I visited many modern school buildings, I felt I had completely failed to find such spaces. They additionally did not have any connection with Japanese cultural inheritance; they would not be able to last as long as classics. While taking tours to 30 or more school buildings and public facilities, I read many books about architecture. Because I was looking for even a tiny trace of my image of spaces in those books, it was not so difficult for me to read special books for professionals. If I did not find such information in a book, I simply moved to the one next.

When I was lost in a forest of modern architecture, I read the Japanese version of *Form Follows Fiasco: Why Modern Architecture*

Hasn't Worked, written by Peter Blake, in which he criticized modern architecture thoroughly. Until then, I had been thinking that a modern society driven by two guiding factors, rationalism and scientific technology, had finished its role already. Then, Peter Blake gave me a final push on my back.

I was thinking a school was very close to "a house to live in," because faculty and students lived everyday there like in a house. A school is a place completely released from the labor pains of earnings. "Going back home" sounds like a kind of release from labor. A school should be a comfortable place to enjoy everyday school life like a house with spaces of sweet memory. An ambiguous image I had about a school seemed to be a so much clearer one; it turned out to be a common aspect of a house with spaces of sweet memory.

When I visited Chris in Berkeley for the first time, I told him that I wanted to have Wright-like schools without giving him any deeper explanation about it. I was thinking of a Campus filled with sweet memories. I felt that my ambiguous image of spaces in our Campus was turning real.

However, it was necessary for me to overcome more tough issues when proceeding with preparatory work with Yasui Architectural Design Company, Ltd.

Homeroom Street

After a tough experience with Yasui, I found Chris at last.

The school requested Yasui to accept our unique proposal and failed. I enjoyed the interesting book written by an architect, *Yada Yoh*, who was a professor at Waseda University, Tokyo. He said:

"Please keep company with an architect and enjoy chatting with wine for three years at least without having any conversation on architecture. Then, three years later, this architect will be able to read your true mind behind your words. Now, while discussing the design of your house, you may request anything you like whenever you think of; the architect will understand what you really want, even when you give this architect ideas that are contradictory to your real will."

When the school decided to ask Yasui for the design of our new Campus, I asked two young architects at Yasui, Hattori and

Odagiri, who had been cooperating with me in visiting school facilities as my preparatory study. So I made a proposal to Yasui. I was thinking about the preparatory work before entering into the actual design work. I wanted architects to grasp what a school is by enjoying chatting with faculty while seeing classes, club activities and even a faculty meeting. Mr. Kurahashi, a principal, also wanted those two young architects from Yasui to follow those activities as an official part of work. I said to them:

"The only condition is not to talk about even a tiny topic of architecture. You are professionals and the faculty is just amateurs. I do not want faculty, amateurs, led to some fixed ideas for a new Campus by you, professionals. The purpose of keeping company with the faculty is just to understand what a school is through conversation with them and through seeing real school activities. Any of the faculty or students is ready to answer any questions you have." In addition, I said: "The school is paying $100,000 to Yasui just for this work."

Because they had never experienced such work, the two architects were interested in this proposal very much and told me that they were trying their best to persuade Yasui to accept it.

However, no response from Yasui came to the school for almost one month, while the faculty and staff were waiting for their visit. Mr. Kurahashi said to me, "What is happening with Yasui?" Finally, I visited Yasui. For the first time, a chief of its sales department came in and said:

"Hattori and Odagiri gave me a report on your idea. I know your proposal as preparatory work before starting the actual designing process. I understand you want them to have conversation or discussion with the faculty. However, I don't understand the 'condition' of not discussing any matter of architecture. You told them that they might enjoy free discussion with the faculty on any school matters, provided that they are not allowed to talk about architecture. What does it mean?"

After I had explained my reasons, he continued: "We, Yasui, are supposed to work on proceeding with the designing process and our staff members are working accordingly. Without talking about architecture, Yasui cannot send our staff members to a client."

I countered that the school wasn't asking Yasui to send their staff members to our school for free. The school is paying $50,000 ($100,000 at today's rate) just for this preparatory work with the faculty. He replied:

"We, Yasui, refuse it. Yasui is receiving money for our designing work. Yasui cannot receive money without doing any design work. We have never received such money up until now. We cannot deal with such a strange request."

He repeated the same words again and again. Our proposal was finally refused. Until that time, I had decided not to ask modern architects to design our Campus. I personally knew Hattori and Odagiri of Yasui very well and thought that those young architects knew how I wanted to proceed with the project. They seemed flexible. So, after becoming real friends with the faculty, I thought we would be able to build our Campus through discussion with them. Except for those young architects, I knew no one else with such a background.

Therefore, I thought of using well-experienced master carpenters. Through continuous discussion with them, as an ordinary and traditional way of building, I had confidence that we could build our Campus with them. I started looking for master carpenters near Tokyo. Most of them were, at that time, organized by big construction companies in Japan. Some of them I found were positive at first. However, soon after knowing the big scale of the project, they refused to work with us. My friends strongly advised me in chorus not to proceed with such a big scale project just with carpenters.

At the time, I accidentally picked up *The Oregon Experiment*, written by Christopher Alexander, from a pile of books on my desk. I did not expect too much, because I had been tired of a lot of such experimental trials in those books until that time. When I began to read it, I felt that he seemed different from any other ordinary modern architects who usually told a client to leave everything to their hands after hearing a client's request. In this book, Chris (hereafter I will call the professor like I used to during my long friendship with him) was trying to establish general rules and principles which could be applied to the relationship between a client and an architect. He proposed *"user participation"* in *The Oregon Experiment*. He described how to proceed with the designing work with the faculties through continuous discussion with them.

I realized that it was just a traditional way of building viable houses in Japan. A client and a carpenter proceeded with their work by continuously discussing with each other. It used to be an ordinary way in Japan. However, it disappeared when modern architecture was introduced and an architect appeared in front of us as a professional. Then, a deep and serious gap between a client and an architect began to grow.

Chris seemed to reestablish this traditional way. I finally felt I might have found the architect I had been looking for until that time. I gave this report to the board and after receiving its approval, I decided to visit him in person in Berkeley, California. Hiro Nakano, one of his students who had just come back from his California office, introduced me to him by an international call.

In Berkeley, Chris listened to me very carefully when I explained the Eishin Project, as well as the tough situation I had experienced after Yasui's refusal. We enjoyed nice discussions and I confirmed that he shared the same idea about architecture as I did. I asked him if he could accept my proposal to be the chief architect for the Eishin Project. He said yes.

Of course, I added: "Please make sure that you work with the one hundred staff and faculty." He promised to and agreed to come to Japan the following April to conclude a contract with the school. As soon as I returned to Japan, I gave the board my idea to choose Chris as the chief architect for the project. As preparatory work to get an agreement from the faculty meeting, I distributed copies of *The Oregon Experiment* written by Christopher Alexander and *Failure of Modern Architecture* written by Peter Blake to all the faculty and staff. After that, the board opened a faculty meeting and agreed on choosing Chris as the chief architect for the project.

Chris came to Japan in April, 1981. When the contract was concluded at the school, Chris made a statement to the board that he would try his best to create a small and beautiful village as a new Campus. I was very happy. I knew that I had hit right on the target … my image about a school was exactly materialized in the wording of a small and beautiful village.

Later on, about 30 journalists and young architects had a small meeting. The main theme of the meeting was user participation and the pattern language. Time went by very fast with interesting questions and answers between Chris and them. Then, a question was posed to me. "What made you choose Christopher Alexander, while there are many other talented architects in Japan?" I answered right away: "I chose Alexander because, first, I knew he shared the same idea about architecture as I did and follows a very *ordinary way of building* as in Japan, which, I am sorry to say, has become very rare

Window and staircase
Library

today. Secondly, I did not want to have a modern architect for the design of our new Campus and I found that he was not a 'modern architect,' but has always been against a stream of modern architecture. I did not choose him because of his fame. Honestly speaking, I did not know he was a well-known architect in the world at all."

The next day, he came to my room at school and said that he had highly appreciated my answer at that small meeting. He added that he was going to publish a book after completing the project and wanted to use *The Ordinary Way* as its title to express his thanks to me.

How the Project Language evolved through interviews between Chris and the faculty

When I introduced the book by Yada Yoh to Chris, he told me that it was impossible to waste three years. Instead, he proceeded with making a pattern language for the project with the faculty to implement user participation through the process. I felt relieved and was looking forward to seeing how he was working with faculty in this process.

Before leaving Japan, Chris asked a land surveyor to make a survey map with a 20 cm contour. Usually, a survey map has a one-meter contour. However, he wanted to leave the original geography of the land as much as he possibly could. He soon began making a small clay site model with Hiro. It was a pleasant surprise for me to see how strongly he focused his attention on the project. Chris wore a white shirt with no tie and cotton pants all through the year. His casual fashion and frank personality worked well to relax the teachers. They were talking about various aspects of school activities and about their dreams of a new Campus. One of the interesting questions Chris asked them was: "What is the most holy place in a school? Let me have your ideas, please." They were embarrassed when faced with this unexpected question. One of the teachers came to me to ask if it was alright for him to say everything he wanted to. I said to him that it was quite okay as long as it was his real desire.

What was the common sense of the school buildings surrounding them today? In their image, all the school buildings were

Classrooms

reinforced concrete boxes. It was almost impossible for them to even imagine a wooden structure for school buildings. It was very hard for them to talk about even a tiny wooden-made classroom, and almost impossible to have an image of a wooden gymnasium. Chris worked hard to break the hard shell that covered them and tried to reach the true desires lying behind them. One of the toughest jobs for Chris was to do this by interviewing them. If not, a record of interviews would just be a collection of fragmental information reflecting a stream of modern architecture today.

For example, Chris talked about the Judo Hall with physical education teachers for several days and came to me with a serious face. He said that he had met with seven physical education teachers, including judo instructors. He wanted to confirm the spiritual aspect of judo with them. As judo turned into a worldwide sport, it completely lost its spiritual aspects. Physical education teachers had lost it, too. Actually, the Judo Hall has stone stairs that reach up to its entrance door, because it is extremely important to build up some feeling of tension when entering traditional judo halls. On the other hand, it is an entrance of an ordinary gymnasium as well ...

Special features of a process of making a Project Language

Every architect may say: "I always pay respect to a client's request and follow it when proceeding with our design work. User participation is not new." An architect usually asks a client for a summary of requests. For instance, if a client is a school, there are many teachers. Listening to their requests one by one could be confusing. Therefore, an architect says to a client: "Please collect requests from them and give me a summary of those requests after putting them in order. I do not want to have confusion with so many kinds of fragmental information." In this process, individual requests are usually rejected and those shared by many people are adopted. When it comes to collecting the so-called individual request, the role of user participation ends. Many individual requests reach a person in charge. After receiving a summary of requests, an architect says to a client, "Now, please leave everything in my hands."

Cafeteria

Except for Chris, there may not be many architects who proceed by interviewing one hundred employees. Actually, Chris did it. Sometimes he talked with teachers for one hour or more. It took a lot of time and energy. A very important point of this process was not to make a list of majority requests from the users. Instead, even an individual idea or a request was picked up in a positive way and such minor ideas could be used to create a Project Language. A homeroom street was proposed only by one lady teacher of biology, Mrs. Tomizu. In Kitakyushu City, Fukuoka Prefecture, they had a kindergarten where small reinforced concrete box rooms for kids were laid out on both sides of a narrow lane. It was very unique. However, we had gotten used to having a "Japanese shopping street" with shops lined up on both sides of a road. Nakamise in Asakusa is another example of famous sightseeing spots in Tokyo, laid out in this same manner. A homeroom street was later so naturally accepted by the students because it was based on such a cultural background, I assume.

A lake arose because of the geographical reason that a low and wet part on the site had very often turned into a swamp after heavy rains. This place was predestined to be a lake if we could listen to a voice of the land. Chris reflected his deep intention toward these types of ideas very much. The current method of civil engineering to flatten levels on the site with bulldozers did not pay any attention whatsoever to such a low and wet part of a site. Those two concepts were born from preserving a natural land form in that region and our deep feeling of sweet memory we had about a historical shopping street, which finally gave the Project Language a reality.

I now summarize:
1. Chris completed individual interviews with one hundred faculty members and students.
2. Through the interviews, Chris and his staff tried to break the hard shell of common sense covering them and reached the true desire hidden behind the hard shell.
3. Teachers gave their requests and ideas about a new Campus, from minor things to what they wanted on the Campus as a whole. The purpose was not just to make a list of the majority opinions and comments.
4. Even if a request only came from one person, it could be picked out in a very positive way as long as it gave the Campus its own life (reality).

5. It was very important to pay attention to the school's educational policy, respecting and growing the individuality of the students and faculty, when implementing a place for their everyday school life like a house to live in.

In the current design work process, such trials as mentioned above are not done. The school did not have any sketch of a new Campus from the outset. Users were not influenced by a fixed image at all. Each stage of design work in the project was completely different from current ones.

In May, Chris came to Japan with the first draft of the Project Language. Takaaki Aida, a geography teacher, said: "It is a poem. It expressed the faculty's true desire about a new Campus in the form of a beautiful poem."

An image of a new Campus as a whole, which came from this poem, was completely different from any kinds of subjective images that architects thought of individually. Because when the draft of the Project Language was introduced to the faculty, many teachers shared and supported the image of this poem. As a result, the draft was accepted by them in a faculty meeting. The first draft was modified three times and the final one approved by the school in June. We entered into the site plan process as the second stage.

The site plan was done on the site itself.

The site for the school was in Iruma City, Saitama Prefecture and its area size was 6.7 hectares. The land was covered with tea bushes and had a slanted slope from west to east. To the east, we could see the long valley where National Route 16 runs through. It had a wet place to the south east of the land, which became a swamp very often after heavy rains. The site plan was done on the site itself with many bamboo sticks with flags, which were used to identify the four corner points of buildings described in the Project Language. We began to make tours to the site. Hajo Neis and Hiro Nakano, who were students of Chris, joined tours with a dozen teachers.

Hosoi's "Secret Window" on the second floor of the Great Hall. Since the window is mostly closed, this view is easily overlooked by visitors.

The first task was to decide where the entrance of the Campus was. The first entrance building (small gate), the main entrance building and the entrance street connecting these two buildings were described in the Project Language. They had to decide on their location. Entering the Campus from the west side was not good because they had to cross the lake after going down a steep slope. One of the ideas could be to enter the Campus from the southeast side. The problem was that they had to climb a very steep cliff to reach the first entrance building. They decided to place the location of the first entrance building in the east-northeast so that the entrance street to the main entrance building was roughly flat. It was quite natural to reach this final decision.

After entering the Campus from the first entrance building (small gate), they would be led to the main entrance building by walking on an 80-meter-long entrance street to a complex of facilities in the central part of the site. Chris explained his idea about the central complex buildings as follows: In the first stage, the location of big buildings (Great Hall, gymnasium, multi-purpose building and Judo Hall) would be decided. Then the locations of smaller ones would be decided by paying attention to a balance of the buildings as a whole. Behind the main entrance building there would be a plaza surrounded by the Great Hall, homeroom street and administration building. The plaza would be open off to the lake. A wooden gym would be placed on the left side of the lake. We would see a cafeteria on top of the hill over the lake.

We used flag sticks to define where to place those buildings on the site. We used blue flag sticks to define the shape of the lake. Regarding the other buildings, different colored flag sticks were used to show their four corner points. We used red flag sticks for the Great Hall, gymnasium, multi-purpose building and Judo Hall. For small buildings like the administration building, the homeroom and faculty buildings, the cafeteria, etc., we used yellow flag sticks to define the four corner points and white to show the center lines between the buildings. It was a lot of fun for the faculty members to walk around the site with Chris and his staff members to decide the location of the buildings. Very often the location of those buildings could be changed by moving flag sticks. Hajo and Hiro were very busy moving flag sticks according to the instructions Chris gave.

After those buildings are actually built, we are unable to see their backs from the plaza. We can't see the faculty buildings and Judo Hall behind the administration building or the gymnasium from the homeroom street. However, because of the magic of the image, we could see the hidden buildings behind the buildings just as an image. It was not an analogical expression that we could grasp those buildings in a central part of the site as a whole. We saw all the buildings as an image. Although the buildings described in the Project Language were not built yet, all of a sudden, from the plaza, we saw how they appeared in front of us as a mirage. It was a wonderful experience we could only enjoy on the site. We, standing on the ground, shared this mirage in common. In other words, it could be called a virtual reality.

Such a mirage is completely different from an image an architect has in his head while proceeding with a site plan at a desk referring to a site map. At a desk in a room, we can neither see blue sky, enjoy a distant view of Mt. Fuji and the other mountains to the west, nor have a view of the valley where National Route 16 runs through. Especially, no tea bushes surrounding the site could be seen in a room.

We walked around ceaselessly, moving flag sticks to adjust the exact location of buildings. A mirage shared by them through the actual site plan, working on the site, was much, much nicer than an image of an architect that came from an individual idea.

It was an unexpectedly pleasant experience which we realized on the site. Regarding the scale, we were surprised to feel the huge volume of the Great Hall and to see the big size of the lake. Outside of this central part are the sports facilities like the soccer field, tennis, volleyball and basketball courts. The layout of these sport facilities was very different from the current, ordinary one where school buildings are laid out along a roadside or pushed away in a corner of the site to get a bigger playing field. The problem is that such a layout results in a cold, desert-like feeling when students are not on a big playing field. It could fall into ruin or become a solitary strip of land. In order to avoid a desert-like feeling, at my request Chris invented a layout that placed a complex of facilities in a central part of the site and the sports fields outside, surrounding this center. Now, visitors will not see such outside sports facilities while walking about the Campus. Even when all of the students are in the classrooms and not on the soccer field or tennis courts, no visitors will see empty sports facilities, nor get a solitary feeling of a desert.

On the site, we worked hard to lay out other small staff buildings according to Chris' advice. One of the very important things through this work was that we could proceed with seeing the

Sitting niche in the Central Hall

surrounding environment as well. Chris carefully dealt with how to generate a harmony of the regional environment and the Campus. A balance of harmony among the facilities of the Campus was important as well.

We enjoyed the wonderful mirage appearing in front of us as the symbol of the work between Chris, his staff members and the faculty. A layout resulting from such a long journey was then drawn down on paper to become the final site plan.

Now, if the necessary system of function is given to an architect, is it alright for him or her to keep thinking about design based on an image and to materialize an individual design just freely? I still can't help wondering how to pay attention to cultural inheritance. A critical point is how to create a new culture over the old one. Historically speaking, would the succeeding culture be an obstacle for our new trials? What about a harmony with the regional environment?

In this project, Chris tried to recover the regional culture, the natural shape of the land, the harmony with the surrounding environment, as well as harmony among facilities on the Campus, which modern architecture abandoned to get freedom for their individual image. From the first stage of making the Project Language, Chris proceeded with the work through continuous discussion with one hundred faculty members and students. It was a typical, traditional way of building houses through discussion between a client and a master carpenter. Such an attempt by Chris, of course, goes against the stream of modern architecture and the current way of construction by big companies in Japan.

The actual work of Chris and faculty on the site with the many bamboo sticks with flags made us once again realize the true meaning of an ordinary way of building houses in the old days in Japan and to see what problems modern architecture has caused today. It is a fact that the process of the ordinary way of building was done on the site through discussion between clients and carpenters. It was a wonderful experience and memory for us to see the 3D mirage of our Campus in the expected future as a nice reward, in spite of the hard, but enjoyable work when we were standing on the place which had supposed to have been a plaza.

Eishin Campus
March 2017

Photographs by Helmut Tezak

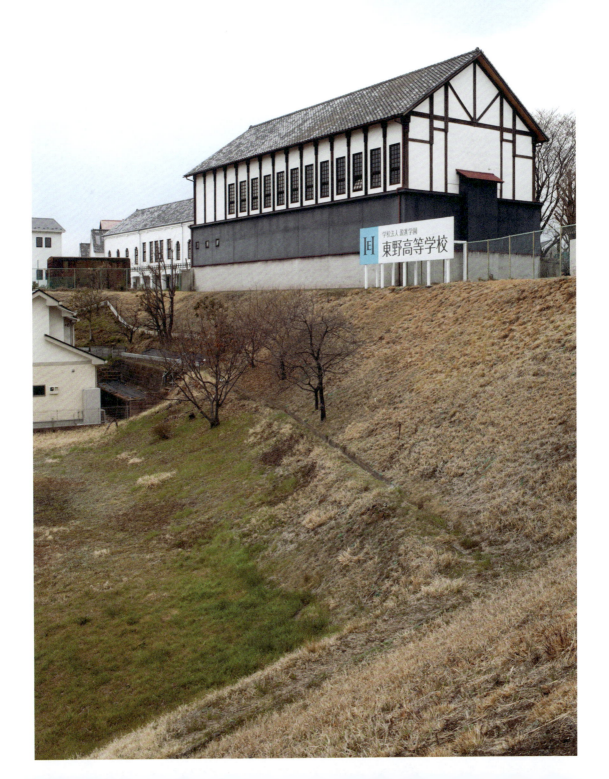

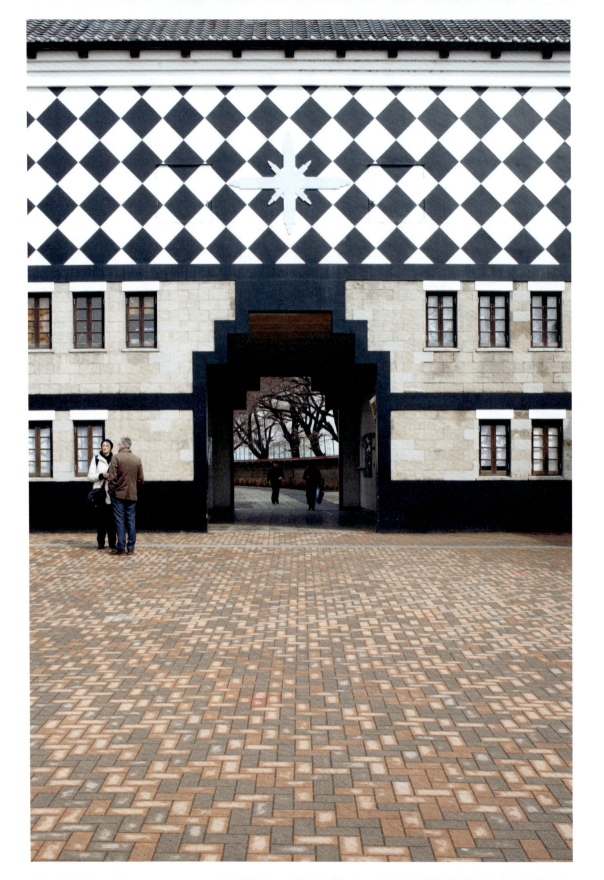

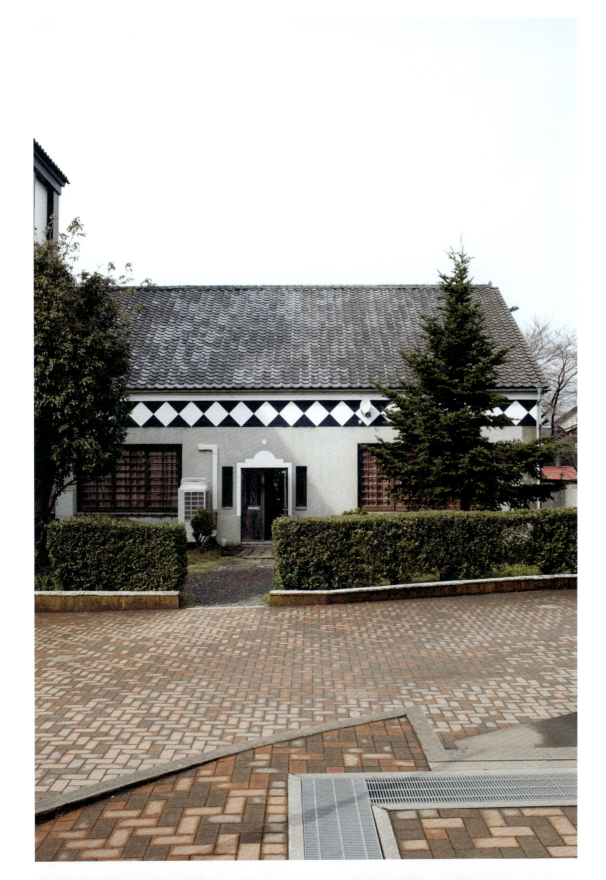

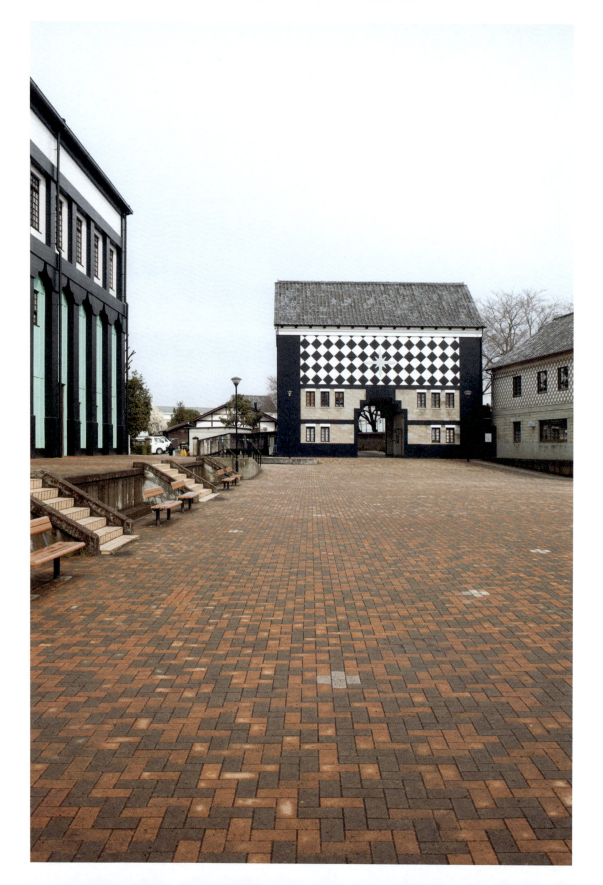

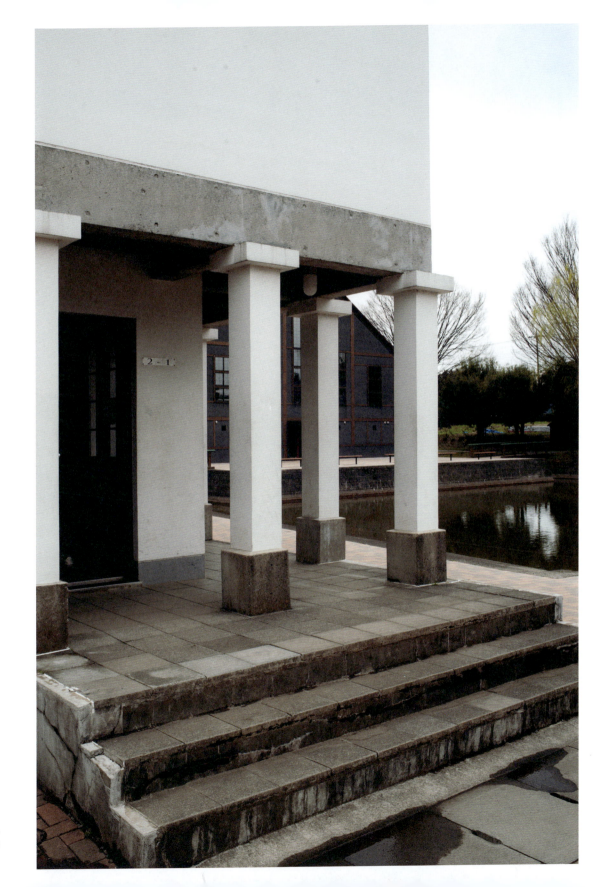

学校法人 盈進学園　東野高等学校

ARCHITECTS: Christopher Alexander, Gary Black, Ingrid F. King, Hajo Neis – CES Center for Environmental Structure, Berkeley

STUDENTS PER YEAR: ~1000

ADDRESS: 112-1 Nihongi, Iruma-shi, Saitama-ken 358-0015, JP

eishin.ac

REALIZED: 1982–1985: Opening April
1985–1987: Extension, color completion and horticultural design – 9, 11, 3, 18

BUILT LATER:
2002: Student Clubhouse
2013: "System B" Clubhouse

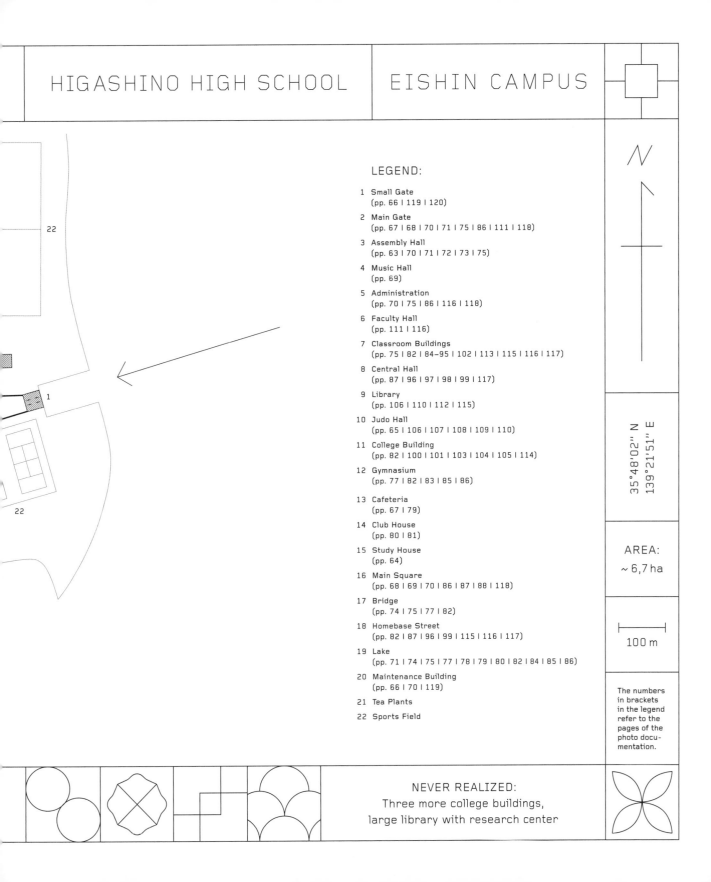

Hajo Neis, Borken, Germany, July 2017

*Shifting Values in Architecture and Urban Design
— A Conversation with Hajo Neis, Borken, July 2017*

> You wrote that the Eishin Campus is your favorite project. We would like to know why this is so and—in a kind of brief overview—how you experienced the preparations, the development process, the implementation, the completion and also the reception of the campus.

Thank you for the opportunity to outline my perspective and experience in the creation and implementation process of the Eishin Campus in Japan. For me, the Eishin project is the culmination of what I wanted to achieve in my architectural and urban design and planning life at the time. Based on the student movement in the 1960s and 1970s in Frankfurt and Darmstadt, it was a long but ultimately successful path to the completed Eishin Campus in 1985. The student movement was intriguing in itself and I learned critical and liberating thinking from the Frankfurt School—as one of Adorno's last students in the summer semester of 1969, as well as in several street battles with the police and in protest actions such as the Taheri extradition protest.

In the end, we in the European student movement failed to create a new architecture and renewed urbanism that could provide fresh opportunities for a better world, not just in the developed world, but all over the globe. The European and German architecture student generation at that time was strongly influenced by the confrontation with the fathers' generation, by social concerns, participation and transparency in public decision-making, house squatting. But it was mostly socio-political activities or liberating actionism, without a true, new, positive architecture in itself, without a new urban development process, perhaps with worthwhile experiments here and there, but nothing fundamentally new with architecture and urban planning as the central core. At the end of the student movement in the mid-1970s, a number of my colleagues—along with the more conservative green fundamentalists—co-founded the Green Party of Germany, and they were also very successful in influencing German politics almost immediately. I myself first turned to developing countries, to African vernacular architectures and settlement structures. In this context, I went to Berkeley for a year to work on my dissertation about East African cities.

Fortunately for me, Chris Alexander was teaching in Berkeley at that time. His teaching aroused the hope of a new urban planning and architecture, as it seemed possible to me in my early student days as a progressive, concrete utopia. In my first major project with Alexander, in 1979, we already developed a completely new theory of urban design and planning based primarily on processes, dynamics, surprise, and guiding principles and ideas such as "Wholeness in the Structure of the City." The book *A New Theory of Urban Design*—the title suggestion is mine—was published in 1987. Here we had a new theory of urban architecture and urban planning which was certainly ahead of its time and probably still is, probably best summarized with the principle of "The City as a Growing Whole." The next step was to translate and transform this progressive theory and make it applicable to current, larger, real-world urban projects. A first attempt for a new city in Venezuela was indeed very promising. Guasare New Town in the Zulia coal-mining region on the Colombian border was a great dynamic growth and development experiment in which we cooperated with Kevin Lynch, whereby Lynch and his team would design the formal mining housing sector while the Alexander team developed the informal sector. However, the oil money ran out in the early 1980s, so after just two years we were obliged to find and engage in another larger project of this kind. The request and subsequent order for the Eishin Campus design in Japan suddenly turned up as a very promising project that seemed ideal in the combination and integration of an urban campus and individual building architecture.

You ask about the preparations for the Eishin project. These are mostly well described in the *Battle* book, beginning with Director Hisae Hosoi's visit to Chris Alexander's home in Berkeley in 1981. He asked if we could apply the two principles of Participation and Pattern Language to all the people involved, as he had learned from the Oregon Experiment book, where Alexander and CES designed a progressive University Campus Plan that is still in use today. Hosoi further requested us to also consider preparing a preliminary design, which should then be continued together with a Japanese architect for the next phases.

From my experience with larger educational projects in my father's architecture office (Hans Ludwig Neis in Siegburg), and my previous experience in Japan, I was soon involved in the Eishin project, and from then on I participated in all important project conversations with Chris and Hosoi. I also started to take care of the practical side of the project in the CES office, first in Berkeley and later in Tokyo as Executive Architect.

If you look at the theoretical and architectural work of Alexander, what is the significance of the Eishin Campus in your view—apart from being the largest realized project?

In the article *"The Generative Urban Code"* in Tigran Haas' book *New Urbanism and Beyond: Designing Cities for the Future,* Chris and several colleagues evaluated various CES projects with a set of criteria for the application of principles and for success in the execution and in the end product. The Eishin Campus was rated very high, but not exactly at the top. Smaller projects such as the Medlock House near Seattle were ahead. How come? I was curious about the reason for this. But in fact, when you think about it, it is not that surprising. Smaller projects can be handled and controlled in a more detailed way than larger or very large projects, especially when you develop a project in the design-build method, and building in the design-build method, and as a building contractor, has always been an important part of CES projects. Here, one should understand the design-build method in its original meaning, which in our case means that the architect not only designs and draws, but also builds directly (sometimes with his own hands). It is quite advantageous to

Christopher Alexander/CES: Medlock House, 1988

implement smaller projects yourself, because you have much more range and scope to experiment, test and complement specific details, which can then be transferred and used to full effect in larger projects. The heavy timber construction in the Gymnasium, Judo Hall, and Central Hall are cases in question, or the two different exterior wall construction systems, one in the Administration Building and the other one in the Main Entrance Building. What you call "apart from being the largest realized project" is still a very critical aspect for me. Not only because of my personal interest in larger projects and urban design, but also because it is a real challenge to achieve qualities of small projects and details in larger projects like Eishin. The practical significance is, therefore, primarily to demonstrate how larger projects can be designed and built according to the theories of Alexander and CES colleagues—with qualities of wholeness in many details as well. On the theoretical level, the value may be even more significant. Here I think of Alexander's description and analysis of the scientific evolution of the last 400 or say even 150 years that has led to a situation where the increasing drifting apart of "facts and values" has led to a situation where cold facts dominate the world more and more than calming and positive constructive values (and these days we are confronted with the perverse and complicating fake facts). However, the Eishin Campus was always intended to be built on principles of value from the outset, to show pupils, educators and parents new, positive opportunities in the development of human interaction and connection with the environment. This has always been the crucial bond that kept teacher Hisae Hosoi and professor Chris Alexander together, I think. The confidence that the future is created humanely much better with values than with facts alone has always held visionaries together—from the Frankfurt School's critical approach to Chris Alexander's humanism and visionary approach in architecture and forward-looking way to create and coexist in the built environment.

How were the roles assigned to the people involved in the Eishin project? On the one hand, we are interested in the participation process, on the other hand, the relationship between Alexander and Hisae Hosoi and the other participants—the teachers, pupils, authorities ...

When you read the *Battle*, you know that there were many different actors in this "thriller." But here I think you are addressing the organized roles and responsibilities of individuals who directed and drove the process. Applying the design principles of *Participation* and *Pattern Language* with all the teachers, students, administrators and other members of the Eishin administration was Hosoi's primary concern from the outset. For him, these two principles presented ideal components for a liberal process and progressive Eishin worldview. It was only by working with Chris Alexander that he started to feel his concern was not only taken seriously, but that there was also solid conviction and great experience. The experience, application and methodology of these two principles (plus other principles) described in the book *The Oregon Experiment* on the dynamic Master Plan at the University of Oregon in the US, were probably the key points in the decision to ask Chris and CES to take the first steps in a long design and construction process.

Christopher Alexander and Hisae Hosoi in the flagged tea fields, 1982

Director Hosoi was an ideal client for a project of this magnitude, because he was always ready to understand, to learn and to enable. What is fundamentally important in projects with new and experimental aspects is the full cooperation and support of an open-minded client. Alexander was the great thinker and "philosopher" who, as a pragmatic idealist, always tried very realistically to apply important principles in building projects and also invent and try out new ones. Among them were principles that went far beyond those of Pattern Language and Participation, such as the *Centering Process*, *Structure Preserving Transformations*, or the *Application of the 15 Geometric Properties*, to name just a few. I myself was more likely the fighter and implementer who wanted to see more than just a new architecture, but who was also interested in the process and application of progressive design and construction methods, including "direct design on the site" or the *Construction Manager* (short CM) method, which became a central component of the design-build method at CES. Hiroshi Nakano was an important communicator who always stood by my side, as an architect and translator, and as a former student of Alexander at Berkeley. He showed considerable understanding for the approach and could make important and valuable connections in Japan. The administrative authorities in Japan were very formal and went according to the book, but we were able to convince them in long communication phases about many aspects of the meaning and purpose of our methods and techniques—at least they let us build.

It is also important to me to positively mention the large construction company Fujita Kogyo. Although they eventually forced us out of the role of design-build and forced us to complete the project with them as the main contractor, they were absolutely capable of doing things quickly and expeditiously, and working with us in day-to-day dialogue. As the responsible architect on the site, I could judge this quite well, being also fully aware at the same time that two worlds were colliding here. The subtitle of the book is called *A Struggle Between Two World-Systems* not for nothing. In a way, I am very grateful to Fujita Kogyo for being willing to engage in this "battle," for only then could the opposites be worked out in an almost dialectical fashion.

The biggest thanks perhaps goes to Master Carpenter Sumiyoshi, who, despite his seventy plus years, supported us in all of our efforts and helped us practically in multiple ways. Sumiyoshi was the best connection to the Japanese building culture and construction industry, and embodied the design and construction in a great tradition in direct application in building design and construction. He understood all the traditional, often complicated Japanese wood joints and could build them too— I still have two very instructive wood joint models in my office today as presents from Sumiyoshi-san. He had tremendously good taste and was able to combine aesthetic and constructive building methods just as well and uniquely as modern designs with traditional carpentry. He detailed the larger wooden bridge over the lake on the Eishin Campus in a beautiful and natural way. In Japan there is what is called "a living treasure." These are people and personalities who carry on the culture. Sumiyoshi-san was certainly such a person and *sensei*.

At the EXPO 1970 in Osaka there was a contribution by Alexander in the American Pavilion. How do you rate the reception in Japan then and now? How would you describe

EXPO 1970 Osaka, Big Roof by Kenzō Tange, with Tower of the Sun by Tarō Okamoto

the exchange between the Japanese and the American-European cultural sphere which, on the one hand, has developed theoretically and, on the other hand, developed practically and architecturally (Eishin Campus, Emoto Building, Sakura Tsutsumi Building). In your opinion, has this transfer been successful and how does it work in a different direction?

The word "cultural transfer" never really came up in our conversations. But let's talk about the exhibition in Osaka first. At that time, as a competitive athlete, I was a member of the youth delegation of the German Federal Government at the EXPO '70 in Osaka, where Japan showed itself to the western world in a very modern garb. It was very impressive: a new economic power introduced itself. Moreover, Japan's metabolism approach revealed a new, modern architecture of its own, expressed in spectacular structures such as the Main Exhibition Hall of the World's Fair by Kenzō Tange.

Alexander was already well-known in Japan for lecturing on his thesis and book *Notes on the Synthesis of Form* and the progressive mathematical design methods he developed. Both were critically acclaimed by architects worldwide—including Kenzō Tange, who nevertheless insisted on more than mathematical design applications.

Alexander took this kind of criticism of the architects very seriously, and consequently wrote the most important critique of his mathematical approach in the often published article *"A City is not a Tree,"* thereby opening new possibilities for his own theory to progress and advance. Based on this critique, he then took architecture and urban planning in their specific manifestations and constituent parts, connections and complex relationships, and developed a new environmental system. These components and connections were then worked out as patterns and, together with all the connections between the patterns, emerged as what we now understand as a Pattern Language. The exhibition in Osaka was the first CES exhibit of Patterns to show this new approach. It was supervised and developed in the CES office by Canadian architect Ron Walkey. Organized in more content-oriented presentations than in purely professional graphics, a new world of elements and systems of how to approach, understand and apply architecture and urban design in everyday life in the built environment started to take shape. It seemed like a combination of well-known daily activities and clear architectural elements and configurations, reassembled and supported by mathematics ("tree and semilattice") and systems theory in an innovative and promising way, always clear, understandable and *down-to-earth*.

But now to your question of cultural transfer: In a way, you can certainly talk about the design and construction of the Eishin Campus in this fashion. But the book *A Pattern Language* is also built-up as a universal system, which can be and is used everywhere in principle, but also in local versions and variations. At the same time, it is also a very precise system because the universal patterns are actually also very specific in their different expressions and cultural variations. Therefore, a pattern is easy to understand because it initially poses a problem that keeps recurring in daily life, then it is followed by a scientific or scholarly discussion, and finally it responds with a fundamental solution that demonstrates the response and application of this problem in a variety of manifestations. Take, for example, Pattern 144, "Bathing Room." Here the problem formulation not only talks about the practical need for bathing and cleaning, but also about the cultural understanding "that bathing as a whole is a much more elemental activity with therapeutic and beneficial side effects" (according to Bernard Rudofsky). If one sees how this pattern is used in many different cultures, especially here in the Japanese bathing culture, then one finds something rather inverse. There is no cultural transfer, but you find yourself back in your own culture, as a part and an example of an even greater culture. This connection between the universal and the specific individual culture also explains, in part, the great success and appeal of *A Pattern Language* as one of the best-selling architecture books in recent history, because it is cross- and trans-cultural. The fact that it involves recent theories of mathematics, and especially systems theory, may be less of a cultural transfer than one perhaps based on ancient Asian philosophy, which states that "everything is connected to everything else." Since you ask, I would like to answer that the specific reception in Japan in 1970 was based on promising, new, progressive architectural design methods. Subsequently, since about 1980 practical CES projects in Japan (Alexander and Neis) have shown what these methods can in effect achieve. This inspired a considerable number of Japanese architects, craftsmen and users to apply these methods in practical design and construction projects. One current question for me is what the next step in the development of quality-oriented architecture and design might look like in Japan. This might include critical issues such as: Is it possible to base architecture and urban planning on non-atomic energy and commence with a democratic and transparent planning process?

The Battle *book has a lot to say about the construction of the Eishin Campus. How "professional" was structural engineering actually (and also from today's perspective) calculated and executed, and what role did it play in the Japanese engineering and building construction tradition, for example, in terms of dimensioning?*

Let's look at this topic in two parts: first from the different building constructions systems, details, and permit approvals, and second from the construction manager method, design-build, the general contractor method, the mixed method and the construction process.

Construction and structural engineering were approached very professionally, because otherwise we would not have received a building permit. This was done in several steps. The structural calculations for the building designs were done in-house in our engineering department with chief engineer Gary Black. However, we also worked with a well-known Japanese engineering professor, Genko Matsui. Finally, the structural department of the large-scale contractor Fujita Kogyo was also involved. It was very thorough. At that time, for example, as a new method

Construction work on the Eishin Campus, 1983, according to various traditional construction methods.

for the structural calculation of buildings, the finite element analysis method was applied in parts of the designs. For Japan, standard practice; however, everything had to be converted into the traditional calculation, because this new, progressive method had not officially been approved yet for building permits. For example, for the three large pure timber buildings, a special permit had to be applied for at the Japanese Seismic Engineering Center. These buildings (Gymnasium, Judo Hall, and Central Hall) had initially been calculated using the *Finite Element Analysis* method. In addition, there were a number of outdated paragraphs in the Japanese building code that no longer had any real meaning at this time. In the Central Hall (Tamokuteki Hall), the code required the beautiful wooden outer wall to be hidden behind very ugly, fire-retardant fin walls. The reason in the code was that the building was more than twelve meters high to the edge of the roof. But the law had been drafted at a time when the extinguisher hoses were only able to fully combat fires up to a height of twelve meters, which was no longer the case at this point in time. We had a number of such cases that had to be negotiated with the building authorities and brought to a good conclusion. It took a lot of patience, meeting time and detailed work, so that these kinds of individual problems did not suddenly put the big picture and wholeness of the project into question … With the subject of building permits, we are already in the range of the construction process, CM method, design-build, the *General Contractor* method, as well as mixed methods. This topic is very important, because it leads us into the field of tension of what is later described as "System A" and "System B."

 In summary, I can say that in the course of construction, we first of all built the project by ourselves in design-build method according to the principle of integrated design, planning and construction. But in the second phase, there was a dispute over which method should be used to complete the project. In the third phase, it was done mostly in the general contractor method, but also mixed with our own methods of construction. I would like to try to illustrate this in a simplified form: For the exterior work, forming the land, land improvements and infrastructural measures, we did not only design and plan as the CES company and organization, but we also built in the construction manager method, which can be described as a form of design-build, where the architect acts as a contractor or works with a construction manager. The second phase can be described as a fierce battle for the construction method itself, where they wrestled and fought about which method this project should be completed in. This battle went back and forth and ended in a mixed method that has not found a real name yet, because it was indeed very mixed and can be best described as a curious compromise. It was this battle over the construction method that significantly contributed to the book title *The Battle*.

The third phase is the actual and real construction process. It was all about getting the Eishin College and High School built; we (CES) with our methods and principles, and Fujita with its methods. One can also describe this as a wild mish-mash. The construction process occupies several chapters in the *Battle* book and is well described. At this point we can perhaps summarize that our quality and value-oriented approach had to meet in daily skirmishes with the business-oriented values of Fujita. In spite of all these problems, one has to say that this overheated mixed method was ultimately successful and we were able to finalize construction of the Eishin Campus in this very short construction period of just nine months, in time for the new school year and the opening of the school.

One more question about the book, which, on the one hand, is very impressive and fascinating to read, but, on the other hand, has many ambivalences and contradictions. Could you perhaps tell us something about the "background" of the book, the intention and the addressees? Why the escalation on System A and B and in this one project?

The original title of the book was a far cry from battle, and it was almost the opposite and much more humble with the title *The Ordinary Way – History of the Design and Construction of the Eishin Campus*. It was intended to fit seamlessly into the titles and themes of the previous CES series books as another statement and analysis of the success and advance of CES's progressive and humanistic design and construction methods, this time with experiments on the Construction Manager method and issues of large-scale production of a CES project. In this case, however, the real events developed quite differently. Instead of an "Ordinary Way" at the end, we had to acknowledge a "Battle." It is understandable that you question the battle or System A and B topic, because it may not really fit into the book series and subject matter of an idealistic and humanistic architecture approach. Nevertheless, considering the idea of pragmatic idealism, which I do, this book also makes perfect sense in a broader perspective of transparent and progressive processes in the design and production of architecture and settlements. It therefore may be understood as follows: The original intention was to show how to successfully design and build larger projects in the overall Pattern Language methodology using the principles of *Participation, Pattern Language, Structure Preserving Transformations, Integrated Design* and *Construction*, and a number of additional principles and methods. However, in the development and process of building, this intention met with considerable resistance, which was not internally driven, but externally, and had a primarily political-economic background. Thus, we could use the CM method only partially and could not fully develop and test it for the benefit of other larger projects. That said, we were quite successful in the site and field work, but more limited in the construction of the buildings, where we had to work with the compromise mixed method. This contrast is an integral part of what we later described as System A and System B, where System A, roughly speaking, works with human, creative, and emancipatory methods in environmental design, and System B works with the technical, machine-mechanical and efficient profit-oriented methods. An answer to how the project could have developed as a full System A version cannot fully be given at this point. Here we have to look ahead to other large projects in the future. For Eishin, all we can say is that a compromise mixed construction method can also achieve a good result, especially when there are external constraints and a willingness that force you to work together as intensely and as well as possible.

Altes Eishin-Schulgebäude in Musashino/Tokio (System B)

    Chris Alexander and I started to explore this complex issue a bit further to figure out what could be done. Although some critics see the idea of System A and B as an unreal construct,

I think one should start investigating central questions for both systems, such as the question of more efficiency in System A or more participation in System B. One can simply continue to develop System A with particular research questions. One should also try to work on the question of how System A and B might be brought together. The development of methods that improve our built environment, the city, buildings, parks, streets and homes, should primarily be based on System A philosophy, as it will allow us to achieve necessary improvements and address fundamental questions about innovative ideas, methods and techniques for a human environment more completely and coherently. From my point of view, we could make good progress by working on real-world challenging projects and embed serious research questions within these large-scale urban projects.

As far as the addressees of the *Battle* book are concerned, they certainly include all those professionals and researchers who are curious and motivated enough to tackle questions on practical aspects for large design and building projects. This includes people from public as well as private interest, cities and companies. It also includes those researchers who try to shed new light on these issues with theoretical approaches and questions, and public and private clients who want to make progress in this direction. This implicates universities and private research interest.

The theories of Christopher Alexander are still being discussed, further developed and transferred to other disciplines. Where do you think these theories are going to develop toward? What do you see as their future relevance? What is the future potential of the Pattern Language for you? Is the Eishin Campus an exemplary embodiment of the possibilities created in the Pattern Language?

Chris Alexander has dedicated his intellectual life to the development of a holistic theory of architecture, or in other words, he has sought to build up a reasoning that spans the relationship between the natural environment, the built environment and the human world. Starting with the observation of everyday life in town and country, he and his colleagues have tried to build

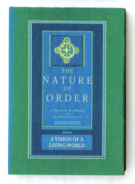

a system that tells us how we can make our environment and buildings more human, functional, beautiful and meaningful. This may be done by starting to work with our own hands; it may also be done in joint design and construction projects, and it can be accomplished based on grassroots ideas and their principles, such as in the procurement of housing for poorer populations. But there is more.

Alexander's grand theory may be understood in two phases: On the one hand, there is the early *Pattern Language* development in the 1960s and 1970s; on the other hand, there is the development of his main work, *The Nature of Order*, from the '80s until about 2004/06, when the four volumes of this opus magnum were published. I myself have been working closely with Chris Alexander since 1978. It can be argued that Pattern Language theory and practice are a well-known and widely used body of work, used and applied in many academic disciplines and professional practices in many different countries. The development potential of Pattern Language is enormous—hence its wide distribution. But considering that the Pattern Language was developed in a time when there was no personal computer, and you still had to work on larger computers with card sets like I had to, you can easily imagine why, in the computer industry, with the personal computer, the adaptations and applications of patterns have taken on gigantic dimensions. Even in the original development of patterns for architecture and urban planning, there are still considerable possibilities for expanding a Pattern Language or Pattern Languages. Updating Pattern Languages to current worldwide sustainability and other critical issues alone is a huge task. If one only considers the digitization of urban systems or the further development of syntax—i.e., the connection of patterns to systems that have dynamic potential—one can try to connect changes in one pattern to changes or modifications in others. So there is still huge potential, in terms of quantity, quality and interrelatedness, especially in interdisciplinary interaction and projects.

Chris Alexander, however, was about more than just developing patterns. He wanted to help to improve the built environment as a whole and discover new ways in which our cities, neighborhoods, streets, green areas, gardens, houses and children's playgrounds could also have a human face in terms of space and human geometry. He has therefore turned to what he calls the nature of order (not: the order of nature), which can be considered as an extension of the Pattern Language, but primarily is also new, spatially oriented and directly related to architecture. The earth is a space and everything we do has to include space. This area of study has more to do with life in space and with space as a quality than just functional configurations and associations. Space in this sense is still largely unexplored in many disciplines, even in our own discipline of architecture and urban planning. However, the potential for development, in its entirety or in particular aspects, is considerable, both in practice and in theoretical work. This process of development in the two major areas of Pattern Language and Nature of Order is already in progress. My own approach is to look at the relationship of these two major areas, but also address important parts. In my lectures, such as *"The Overall Pattern Language Approach,"* I try to address both major areas together. Since 2008/9, I've organized an international conference every two years that deals with critical aspects within this large topic and theory. In this development, the proportion of Pattern Language participants from other disciplines beyond architecture and urban planning is getting larger, so that since 2015 I have engaged with Professor Peter Baumgartner from the Danube University Krems in an arrangement where the conference takes place one year in the USA and in the following year in Austria (PUARL and PURPLSOC). These are just a few examples of current development showing ways into the future of Pattern Language. Coming back to the Eishin Campus in Japan, I would say that the Eishin Campus is not just an exemplary embodiment of the possibilities inherent in the Pattern Language, but rather a *foreshadowing* of potential in both major areas, with the principles of the *Pattern Language,* and much more in the far-reaching principles of *The Nature of Order.*

http://puarl.uoregon.edu/
http://purplsoc.org

Hajo Neis, Yoko Kitamura, 2012

Ms. Kitamura, the current director of the campus, has told us that while there is no direct personal contact with Alexander, there is contact to you. Have you been involved in its adaptation/ expansion or redevelopment in all the years since the completion of the campus?

It should not be forgotten that after the first phase of the construction process in 1985, I stayed in Japan for another five years and worked, designed and continued to build and expand the Eishin project. At the same time, I also worked on other projects, such as the Emoto Apartment Building in the center of Tokyo (with Alexander) or the Sakura Tsutsumi Building on the western periphery (Hajo Neis).

Further work on the Campus 1985–1987 (blue areas), from *Shin Kenchiku* 1987.7

The new work on the Eishin Campus after the first phase of 1985 consisted essentially of parts that had not been built up to then. They included the first two elongated university buildings on the southern Eishin site, as well as improvements to existing buildings—especially the color scheme of old Japanese Shikui plaster in the interior of the Great Hall, and the exterior design of the high school street, also called Homebase Street, as a garden landscape. These were very worthwhile projects that greatly improved the functionality and beauty of the campus for everyday use and made it experientially richer. Here we also designed and built smaller outbuildings in the green outer precinct zone with our own hands. This work was published in 1987 in an article appearing in *Shin Kenchiku*. In 1990 I answered a call to the University of California, Berkeley, but also continued to keep and run the office in Japan until around 2000. Subsequently, I set up exchange programs with the Japanese universities of Meiji and Keio in Tokyo that bring me to Japan every few years and connect me with visits to the Eishin Campus, often with American student groups. I also do sketches and design suggestions for improving the campus, which I then make available, such as a sketch for a green area with a closed row of trees on the college grounds to create better space.

Garden design on Homebase Street, 1987

Great Hall with traditional Japanese color scheme, 1985–87

In the global design-build movement of recent years, do you see a certain affirmation of the direction that Alexander, CES and you have always been concerned about? Does it seem legitimate to you to confirm a tradition here?

Thank you very much for asking me this question at the end, because essentially all CES projects are more or less, mostly more, planned and created in design-build. We can complete the big arch of our conversation with this appropriate topic.

Chris, I believe, always had the entire architecture of the world in mind. Once he asked us in a seminar about how many buildings might actually be around in the world, because after all, we, as architects, are responsible for the buildings of this world and their environment. And considering that there are currently about seven billion people living on Earth, you could perhaps make a simplified calculation: Let's say for every building we count three-and-a-half people, which would amount to two billion buildings. Of these two billion—and this includes all the buildings of so-called slums, favelas and illegal settlements—roughly ninety percent are built in a simple manner and mostly self-built; only about five to ten percent are planned by architects and engineers.

What I'm saying is that this is not just a one-off solution, but a new and wide perspective for two billion and more buildings, and for seven billion people, and these seven billion people will grow to at least ten billion by the middle of the century. This would bring about another billion new buildings, so that we reach about three billion. A gigantic number. Of these three billion, many have to be built new, or rebuilt, many must be remodeled, repaired and maintained, which is a huge challenge in itself. From this point of view, we can talk about a simplified form of design-build, which is already a bigger producer in the built-world than the professionally organized construction industry system.

Rio de Janeiro – Cityscape characterized by self-construction, architectural buildings and design-build

The question is how to use design-build and self-help construction to create livable and living space and also help to develop building cultures that bring diversity, wealth and possibly even the love of buildings. This question does not only apply to developing countries, but also to countries in Europe. In Poland, for example, 3.7 million residential units are missing, making it very difficult for young people to start a family. In the meantime, some are thinking about how forms of design-build could help close the gap here. This cannot be done by architects alone, but requires a wide range of actors who have to tackle such a task from the ground up. What I have called the *Overall Pattern Language Approach* can help to form an essential foundation for a broad-based, design-build culture that puts the built environment on many solid feet, and considers it more in-depth as a value per se which, in day-to-day planning and building, has to be found and recovered again and again. In doing so, the principles of the Pattern Language and the principles of the extended Pattern Language in the form of the *Nature of Order* can continue to provide considerable assistance. Here I would like to refer in particular to Volume 3 of the *Nature of Order* book, *"A Vision of a Living World,"* which deals with practical CES projects, and is full of projects of all kinds, with different topics, contexts, types and questions, but also with different orders of magnitude, starting from construction detail all the way to whole cities. *"Levels of scale"* matter!

Claudia Mazanek, Hajo Neis, Eva Guttmann, Borken, July 2017

Christian Kühn
The Pattern Language for the Eishin Campus

Anyone who studies Christopher Alexander's architecture and architectural theory must have no reservations about esotericism. Alexander is always concerned with the whole, whereby the proximity of the term "whole" to the term "healing" plays a central role.

"[...] the idea of wholeness encompasses the idea of healing. When something is whole, we consider it healed. If we wish to heal something, we seek to make it whole."[1]

There is more than enough to heal in the built environment, as Alexander perceives it. Among his references is "The Waste Land," the 1922 poem of the American-English writer and Nobel laureate T. S. Eliot, whose criticism of civilization Alexander shares.[2] The battle for the life and beauty of the world, which provided the title to his latest book, is in full swing for Alexander, and architecture is, in his view, the decisive discipline when it comes to creating a new, holistic civilization:

"The foundations of this new civilization must be rooted in its architecture. It requires an architecture for real life—a new physical structure. That means a new arrangement of physical forms, spaces, buildings, the shapes of buildings and the shapes of spaces, and, above all, a new and realistic philosophy of arranging gardens and streets, and a new philosophy of building them."[3]

For Alexander, the Eishin Campus was not simply the biggest construction project of his career, but the first chance to realize this architecture of a new civilization, one for which he had formulated the theoretical foundations and implemented some smaller, experimental projects in the years before, on a larger scale. A congenial client was found in the person of Hisae Hosoi, who wanted

---

[1] Christopher Alexander et al., *The Battle for the Life and Beauty of the Earth. A Struggle Between Two World Systems,* (Center for Environmental Structure, Book 16), New York: Oxford University Press, 2012, 89. In his earlier writings (prior to the four-volume review *The Nature of Order: An Essay on the Art of Building and the Nature of the Universe,* Berkeley, CA: The Center for Environmental Structure; 2001–2005). Alexander avoided the term "wholeness," but instead spoke of a "quality without a name," which escapes every definition in the best esoteric tradition, but is accessible to intuition; cf. Alexander, *The Timeless Way of Building,* New York: Oxford University Press, 1979, IX.

[2] *The Battle,* as of 78ff several quotes from "The Waste Land."

[3] *The Battle,* 476.

to achieve the same objective as Alexander, the construction of a new civilization, through education. The Eishin Campus was to include a private secondary school and a science university, supplemented by a research center and a library.

Influenced by the ideas of John Dewey, the American pragmatic philosopher and founder of the University of Chicago Laboratory School, Hosoi wanted to run his school as a laboratory of democracy. The participation of all those involved was a matter of course for him, which, however, was not adequately supported by the Japanese architects he approached. Inviting Christopher Alexander was therefore an obvious choice, despite the great geographical distance. Not only did Alexander advocate a radically participatory idea of the "making of buildings," but he also offered an elaborate method, the Pattern Language, which enables users to design according to their own ideas with the help of the architects. The term "Pattern Language" refers, on one hand, to the method developed by Alexander, and, on the other hand, to its best-known implementation in the form of a book that Alexander worked on with several colleagues at the Center for Environmental Structure (CES) in the late 1960s and published in 1977.[4]

In order to better understand the principle of pattern language, a short digression to Alexander's first independent book, *Notes on the Synthesis of Form,* which appeared in 1964 and builds upon his dissertation, is worthwhile.[5] The title of the book is misleading: It deals primarily with the problem of the correct analysis of planning tasks, which, for Alexander, entails subdividing the overall task into solvable sub-problems that are as independent from each other as possible. In view of the dramatically higher complexity of construction tasks under the conditions of modern, open societies, this division can no longer be afforded through conventional methods. The planners would no longer try to get to the bottom of a problem, but rely on stereotypes, often in combination with formal extravaganzas that do nothing to solve the problem.

Alexander therefore suggests using a computer, which receives the relationships between the individual sub-problems as an input, for this task. A subdivision into groups of sub-problems as independent from each other as possible is calculated from these inputs. In the next step, partial solutions are found for these groups and displayed as diagrams that visualize the solution approach. Alexander calls them "constructive diagrams" because they communicate the

[4] Christopher Alexander et al., *A Pattern Language*, New York: Oxford University Press, 1977

[5] Christopher Alexander, *Notes on the Synthesis of Form,* Cambridge, MA: Harvard University Press, 1964.

problem and solution simultaneously. The combination of these diagrams then creates a complete solution for the construction task, a bottom-up process that mirrors the top-down process of problem analysis.

Alexander's concern in *Notes* is not the overcoming of rationalism in architecture, but an attempt to give it a new, methodologically sound basis and to defend it in the interests of users against stereotypical solutions and formal arbitrariness. The pattern language developed by Alexander and his partners at the CES in Berkeley continues this project, albeit with one important difference: While in *Notes* Alexander assumes a hierarchical tree structure in which both problems and solutions are organized, he now speaks of a network of interconnected constructive diagrams, which he renames as "patterns." And while he assumes a calculability of at least the grouping of the sub-problems in *Notes*, he understands the Pattern Language as a distillate of collective experience that can be developed entirely without computer support and in large parts intuitively.

This applies to the pattern language as the method used for the Eishin Campus, as well as the book of the same name. In the book, each pattern begins with a title page featuring the name of the pattern and a photograph that visualizes an archetypal solution. This is followed by a brief introductory problem, then by a detailed discussion of the relevant parameters and possible implementations, usually supplemented by diagrams. At the end there is a concisely formulated instruction that directly addresses the reader. Patterns are additionally subdivided into three classes, indicated in the title by the addition of stars: Two stars denote patterns which the authors assign universal validity to, while patterns with one or no star have less weight. Each pattern is framed by references to others, with superordinate patterns being referenced at the very beginning, and those that serve to refine it at the end. Together, these patterns form a network that can be entered at any point and then forwards the reader through the links.

The topics covered range from urban planning to detailed design. The 253 patterns of the book are arranged from the largest to the smallest. From 1 "Independent Regions" it goes further into detail—to name just a few examples—via 8 "Mosaic of Subcultures," 59 "Quiet Backs," 63 "Dancing in the Street," 66 "Holy Ground," 74 "Animals," 75 "The Family," 125 "Stair Seats," 167 "Six-Foot Balcony," 208 "Gradual Stiffening," until the series ends with number 253 "Things from Your Life." Obviously, this is not a classification by component: Things, spatial situations, activities and abstract concepts are treated as equivalent, architecturally relevant facts under the umbrella term of the pattern.

As Alexander explains in the supplementary volume, *The Timeless Way of Building,* published in 1979, the *Pattern Language* is not just a collection of examples, but a frontal attack on the professionalized form of architectural production. As a design method for the "making of buildings," the pattern language should give the power over the design of their environment back to the users and enable them, building upon a vocabulary of archetypes understood as universal, to not only express their needs, but also to enter into a discourse about possible solutions. In doing so, it goes far beyond what is understood by the term "participation," that is, the users taking part in a design process that is still the responsibility of architects.

Alexander developed a specific pattern language for the Eishin Campus together with the users. The one published by the CES serves, on one hand, as a general reference; on one other hand, a few patterns are also implemented directly in the Eishin Campus. The patterns of learning that are actually relevant to the building task, 18 "Network of Learning" and 85 "Shopfront Schools," are not used because they assume conditions that are incompatible with the idea of a closed campus.[6]

The pattern language for the Eishin Campus, which Alexander published with his wife Maggie Moore Alexander and Hajo Neis in a 2012 book,[7] is divided into eight sections with a total of 110 patterns. The first section describes the "global character" of the Campus, which is characterized by the division into a densely built inner precinct and a largely undeveloped outer one. The educational and university uses lie in the inner precinct, while the recreational and sports areas as well as agriculturally used areas are located in the outer precinct. The further sections roughly follow the division into areas: one section each for the buildings, the streets and the features of the inner precinct, one for the outer precinct, one for special details in the outdoor space, as well as one for the character of the interiors in the buildings. The fact that this structure leads to overlaps is clear and also desired. The length of the individual patterns ranges from a terse *"There is a Soccer Field"*[8] to the detailed description of atmospheres: *"Inside, here and there throughout the Campus, there are surprising*

The arrangement of the two-story classroom houses along a street has a formal, but no functional relationship to pattern 85.

6 ─────────────

7 ─────────────

The Battle, Chapter 9, "A Pattern Language for the Community," 131–152

Ibid., 142

8 ─────────────

*soft highlights of color, shining out among the subdued colors of the rest [...]."*⁹ Most patterns cite the names of people who developed them. In the section on special details in the outdoor space, there is one that comes from Hisae Hosoi and documents the openness of the pattern methods for irritation:

*"There is also one garden, so secret, that it does not appear on any map. The importance of the pattern, is that it never must be publicly announced, must not be in site plan; except for a few, nobody should be able to find it."*¹⁰

Another pattern, which traces back to Hosoi, requires numerous mirrors on the Campus that enable the students to look at themselves. In the description, Hosoi points out how happy students were looking at themselves in the mirror in front of his office. Obviously, mirrors would have a value for the students and, therefore, a separate pattern should be dedicated to them.¹¹

The basis for this pattern language was a process of conversations with students, teachers and administrators that took more than four months.¹² Alexander reports that this process was not without tensions, although not comparable to those that occurred later in the execution. The talks were to not generate proposals for improvements in the status quo, but basically new approaches. The interviewed teachers and students were asked to close their eyes and imagine a paradise in which all their wishes for good teaching and learning could be fulfilled, and to dream.¹³ Not all participants wanted to engage in this process and rather found it to be a distraction from a goal-oriented approach. For Alexander, the result summarized in *A Pattern Language* is not the result of sociological field research,¹⁴ but a work of art in itself:

*"Once again, it must be emphasized that this pattern language is a work of creation, like a poem, created by the architect, but nourished and inspired by the dreams of the users."*¹⁵

For the most part, the drawings that accompanied this pattern language have not been preserved. In his report, Alexander publishes a single sketch from this phase showing the entire system and functional areas. The separation into an inner and an outer precinct is clearly visible. Traversing the outer precinct like an umbilical cord, the entrance road connects the Campus interior with the outside world. The outer precinct appears empty; only the gym and an area of forest are specially marked. Coming from the entrance, one first

---

9 Ibid., 151.

10 Ibid., 149.

11 Ibid., 150.

12 Ibid., 117.

13 Ibid., 118.

14 Ibid., 123.

15 Ibid., 132.

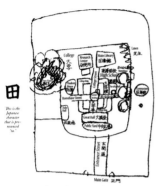

A first idea sketch by Mr. Hagiwara, based on the Japanese character for "ta"; from *The Battle*, 136

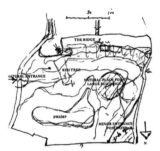

Diagram about the most important topographical centers; from: *The Battle*, 171

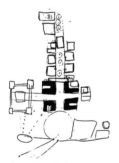

Diagram with the most important centers of the Pattern Language (Entrance Street, Main Square, Tanoji Center, Individual Classroom Buildings with Homebase Street, Library and Research Center, College Buildings); *The Battle*, 170

reaches a public yard where a large event hall stands. A round-shaped main building, surrounded by the square of the university, is located in the center of the inner precinct. The school, with its classrooms, is situated at the side of the area between this square and the outer precinct border. The most contemplative areas, the research center and library, lie farthest from the entrance.

Moreover, the sizes of the individual areas are not exactly defined at this time. In the next step, they will be roughly defined on the basis of the pattern language, calculated using reference projects and balanced with the available budget. The result is a rough space allocation plan with floor space specifications as a supplement to the functional description in the pattern language.

As a further parameter, the site now comes into play. For Alexander, the potential of the site is equally important to the formal solution as the functional specification in the pattern language. Natural midpoints or centers that need to be aligned with those the pattern language requires can also be seen on the site. Of particular importance in this specific case is a terrain ridge located in the very south of the slightly north-sloping pocket of land, and a swampy area in the north, which will transform into a pond in the further planning process. Both aspects of the task are shown in the illustrations. The potential of the location is inscribed in the sketch of the terrain: the most favorable point for the main entrance, the ridge terrain; the natural place for large buildings, the swamp. The sketch of the building featured an initial further development of the diagram from the pattern language: The entrance leads to an open space, the Great Hall is arranged on the right hand side, while the path along the main axis first leads to the center, which is now divided into four buildings, and then straight on to the *homebases* of the school. The research center and library are connected across the transverse axis and form a square that is approximately equal in size to the center.

The next design step ultimately leads to the solution which essentially defines the execution. As suggested in the sketch of the site, the entrance is moved to the east side. It leads as a slightly curved road space flanked by walls with two gates to the public square. The Great Hall lies on the right side while the main axis begins on the left, marked by the school's two-story classroom buildings, and leads to the Central Building, which has no fixed function. It serves as an informal meeting place at the interface between the school and the university. It is covered, but at the same time open to the outside,

Map of the largely realized Campus; from *The Battle*, 200

16 ─────────────
Ibid., 325.

Seating steps in the open alcove, Central Hall

Ibid., 426.
17 ─────────────

because on each longitudinal side there are five gate-like passageways with seating steps in the thick but hollow walls, which are based on the patterns 180 "Window Place" and 197 "Thick Walls" derived from the *Pattern Language*. Illuminated by two skylights located near the roof crown and a narrow, high window at each end, this space gains a spiritual dimension.

Since the Campus was finally built without the university wing and the combination of research center and library, it remains a torso in which the halls seem oversized for events and sports. The Great Hall and Sports Hall were the largest wooden structures built in Japan during the 20th century,[16] and the separate Judo Hall is also a considerable expense. All school and college buildings are connected at least on one side by colonnades, which serve not only to protect against heat and rain, but also as informal meeting places.

Alexander emphasizes that the design process has not yielded a final result up to this point, but only the basis for a gradual implementation in which changes can be continuously made. It was to be expected that this approach would lead to conflicts with the construction companies carrying out the work. Alexander hoped that the incremental process in which the planning and execution take place in detail at the same time would be an approximation to the qualities of anonymous architecture that often lives from small deviations or spontaneous variations of a theme. For the construction companies, Alexander's desire to cast the columns for more than 200 meters of colonnades individually and not to execute them as prefabricated components was a supposed absurdity which they refused to carry out. For Alexander, an essential aspect of architecture was lost, one that had less to do with the love of craftsmanship than with his consideration that a "living" architecture would not be compatible with such mechanical reproduction.

"The extent to which a configuration has life or unity within itself, is caused by the geometrical connections among its elements, and also by its relation to its immediate surroundings. [...] The quality of any building is, to a much deeper degree than we have understood, so far, caused by combinations of these properties that are purely geometric."[17]

In his multi-volume work *The Nature of Order*, Alexander names fifteen of these qualities which he sees as triggering the intuitively felt sense of wholeness. Although his theory seems to dissolve into the esoteric at this point, it nonetheless remains stimulating when

Cf. ibid., 427.
18

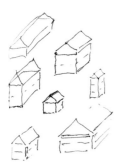

Examples of the different Campus building types; from *The Battle*, 215

terms such as "roughness," "echoes," or "deep-interlock and ambiguity" are discussed as geometrical properties.[18]

On the contrary, the architecture of the buildings on the Eishin Campus falls short of the expectations one may have after reading Alexander's writings. As poetic and precise his specification for the Campus's entire system may be: Alexander does not seem to know any other concept for the building than the primeval hut in the form of a decorated shed with a pitched roof. On the Campus it adopts numerous sizes and proportions that in reality seem stereotyped, like paper models of anonymous architectures from 16th century Elizabethan England, decorated with clunky ornaments.

Why "living" architecture is not able to develop beyond this type cannot be explained by Alexander's theory. His architecture burdens itself with the task of having to invent a radically new architecture with the formal means of the past. The entire potential of spatial strategies built up by the architecture of modernity thus remains unused without deeper explanation. The thought experiment of letting other architects of recent history implement the pattern language for the Eishin Campus must be allowed: What would the result look like if Frank Lloyd Wright or Rudolph M. Schindler had stepped in as architects to translate the pattern language for the Eishin Campus into their architectural language?

Ida Pirstinger
Urban Order and the Ambivalence of the Patterns
On Christopher Alexander's Contribution to the Urban Planning Discourse

Christopher Alexander: "A City is Not a Tree," *Architectural Forum,* Vol. 122, No. 1, April 1965, 58–62 (Part I), Vol. 122, No. 2, May 1965, 58–62 (Part II).

1 ─────────

The city is the most complex of all human artifacts. It is not simply a multi-dimensional, space-giving structure, but above all a complex organizational form of human coexistence. The comparison with a complicated machine may be a helpful abstraction, but it nowhere near does justice to its nature. Rather as a mechanically functioning construct, it resembles a metabolism, because it lives on constant change and must be fed, with matter, with human interactions, new ideas and, indeed, with inconsistencies as well. Although people have been building and living in cities for millennia, there is substantial lack of clarity about the interplay of social, cultural, psychological, structural and other factors of influence. Whereas until the beginning of the 20th century, at least in Europe, urban structures were created, in which we still enjoy living today, later developments are often perceived as controversial or negative and are called anti-urban. Since the beginning of modernity, the new and future urban developments have proven to a considerable extent to be unfit for the emergence of a livable and diverse city. Instead, they cause sprawl, an excess of motorized private transport and steadily growing infrastructure needs with decidedly negative economic and environmental side effects. The limits of urban planning can no longer be concealed. In the diction of Marc Augé, we continue to create characterless non-places without special identity, relation and history, although criticism of this already began to be articulated in the late 1950s.

When Christopher Alexander caused a sensation internationally in 1965 with his text *"A City is Not a Tree,"*[1] he joined a movement that criticized the contemporary concept of urbanity with various means and methods, but also tried to decode the complexity of the city and point out solutions for future better development.

Functionality and efficiency in urban planning, the loosened, structured and functionally mixed, car-friendly city of modernity were just as openly questioned as modernist urban renewal projects in old town areas. Instead, one sought to get to the bottom of the true needs of the people and the structural and architectural secrets of the pre-industrial old cities perceived as being much better. The contribution of New York journalist and activist Jane Jacobs[2] and her standard work, *The Death and Life of Great American Cities* (1961),[3] which is still valid today, cannot be appreciated highly enough. She admittedly did not provide any scientific tools or directly usable solution approaches, but she offered comprehensive food for thought on the physical and design aspects of public space, as well as on the social and economic factors that determine urban life. Her analysis and critique serve as the initial impetus for the further exploration of the topic and as the birth of social-psychological urban criticism, as well as complexity theory and environmental design in architecture and urban planning. Since then we have been aware that city is organized complexity.

At about the same time in *The Image of the City* (1960),[4] the American urban planner Kevin Lynch described five basic urban space-defining elements that city users apply to generate cognitive city maps and record cities. It is a "first intersubjective scientific-psychological methodology of urban design,"[5] based on the perceptual experience of users, where factors such as memorability and readability play a more significant role than the objective, functional requirements of the object to be designed.

Together with his wife Ingrid, a psychologist, the Danish urban researcher and urban planner Jan Gehl has to be regarded as a pioneer in deciphering the connections between urban space and urban life. In 1965, as part of a research and travel scholarship, they began investigating human behavior in the public spaces of Italian old cities—as an inspiration for better planning than the usual lifeless suburbs of Denmark. This led over the course of decades to the emergence of derivations and methods for scientific work in urban research and planning practice, with the highest principle of always focusing on people.

In a 2010 interview,[6] Jan Gehl expressed surprise that so few people have done intensive research on these issues since Jane Jacobs' impulse. Besides William H. Whyte, Donald Appleyard and Allan B. Jacobs, who are listed as references in his books along with several other protagonists, he also expressly names Christopher

---

[1] First authoritative critical publication: William H. Whyte, Jane Jacobs, Francis Bello, Seymour Freedgood, and Daniel Seligman, *The Exploding Metropolis. A Study of the Assault on Urbanism and How Our Cities Can Resist It,* New York: Doubleday Anchor Books, 1958.

[2]

[3] Jane Jacobs, *The Death and Life of Great American Cities,* New York: Vintage Books, 1961.

[4] Kevin Lynch, *The Image of the City, Cambridge,* MA: The MIT Press, 1960.

[5] Helmut Winter, *Zum Wandel der Schönheitsvorstellungen im modernen Städtebau. Die Bedeutung psychologischer Theorien für das architektonische Denken,* Diss., ETH Zurich, 1986, 327.

[6] Greg Lindsay, https://www.fastcompany.com/1689519/cities-people-qa-architect-jan-gehl [Accessed 06.01.2019].

"Urban Design – A List of Key Words: The 12 Criteria," from: Jan Gehl, *Life Between Buildings* (1971), Washington, DC: Island Press, 2011

Alexander. Much of the aforementioned research on the interactions between humans and urban space has retained its relevance to this day. But how does Christopher Alexander in particular position himself in the context of the urban planning discourse back then and today, and how does his work radiate onto current happenings in urban development?

There are hardly any significant urban development projects by Christopher Alexander, on the basis of which his theses on urbanity could be examined. Urbanistic thinking manifests itself primarily in the written theoretical examination of architecture. Christopher Alexander's theories are based on the Design Methods Movement of the early 1960s emanating from Great Britain and the USA. The aim was to objectify and rationalize the previously intuition-driven or trial-and-error-based design processes towards a transparent planning system consisting of systematic design methods and processes using new technologies. Despite all implicit criticism of modernism, this approach remains a profoundly modern one, since it strives, like modernity, for the renewal of society and sees the key to the improvement of the world in objectification and in optimized design methods. A part of the ambivalence in the person and the work of the mathematician and architect Alexander already come to light herein, but also as in Alexander's sticking to these goals and contents after the failure and dissolution of the movement.

Because they are the ones most cited, his most influential writings are probably *A Pattern Language* (1977)[7] and *"A City is Not a Tree."* Inspired by Jane Jacobs' critique, which he calls "excellent," Alexander attempts to comprehend and describe the city's abstract principle of order using scientific and mathematical means in *"A City is Not a Tree."* He divides the city into subsystems, relates them to each other, and concludes that the structures of the planned modern cities do not have nearly the same complexity as the much livelier "natural" cities. Structurally and organizationally, these form a semi-lattice and have considerably more connections between individual parts and subsystems, i.e., subsets and intersecting sets, than the rather linear, hierarchically structured functional city, which resembles a branching tree structure. Suggestions for planning a lively city are not included, but the criticism of attempts to want to create it by deliberately imitating the "accidental" appearance of old urban elements is—a proposition he ascribes to Jane Jacobs.

[7] Christopher Alexander et al., *A Pattern Language*, New York: Oxford University Press, 1977.

A Pattern Language, one of the best-selling architecture books in history, is a system for describing individual architectural and urban design elements or qualities, from the regional scale to the ornament. It is conceived as a practical, hierarchical modular system to better understand the "grammar" of our built environment and, in a holistic sense, is to help build in an objectively good and human manner, but is not to be understood as a list of solutions. Especially in the inextricably linked explanatory text *The Timeless Way of Building* (1979), it is described as a participatory process to analyze emerging problems, to locate and structure existing mechanisms, and to find archetypal solutions that are to be best implemented according to the hands-on principle. The basic idea is that everyone can design and construct a building for themselves.

Christopher Alexander tries to get to the bottom of the collective pattern in old cities and buildings, which is said to have originated from a collective intelligence and stands for an "eternal" and "ego-free" "quality without a name" which has been lost in modern architecture, but which all would deeply have inside them. This quality could only be achieved through a joint, step-by-step approach, which was tested in numerous projects. Although they are precise, the patterns should not be mechanically applied. As Hermann Czech writes in the epilogue to the German translation: *"Patterns are not 'rules,' but structures of arguments."*[8] They are highly adaptable and expandable according to the need and task. Christopher Alexander repeatedly emphasized this, but that was also often overlooked, which could be due to the quite conclusive and definite-seeming tone of his writings. Although clearly focused on the building as a whole, at least 125 of the total of 253 patterns deal with elements of the city and its subunits, such as neighborhoods or the relationship between the building and the environment.

Of all things, the patterns that are not clearly attributable to the context of the region and the city, but to the transition between public and private, appear as the most substantial ones. A few borrowings and cross-references to the work of the contemporaries are to be located here, proof of the attention and recognition that they gave each other. The statement in Pattern 98 "Circulation Realms" is corroborated by Kevin Lynch's description of disorientation in modern cities. Donald Appleyard's realization that too much traffic interferes with the identification of the road space and the buildings lining it found its way into Pattern 14 "Identifiable Neighborhood." The edge

Pattern 160 "Building Edge," from: *A Pattern Language,* 752–756

8 ──────────

Hermann Czech, "Nachwort des Herausgebers," Alexander et al., *Eine Muster-Sprache,* Vienna: Löcker Verlag, 1995, 1265.

St. John's College, Cambridge by Loggan 1690, illustration in Pattern 98 "Circulation Realms," from: *A Pattern Language,* 518

effect described by Jan Gehl,[9] according to which people prefer to stay along the edges of open spaces rather than in their midst, is directly related to patterns 160 "Building Edges" and 124 "Activity Pockets."

Despite global renown as a theorem, the pattern language has hardly prevailed in planning practice, neither for objects and even less for urban planning issues. However, at least as far as the approach is concerned, it is certainly present as an aid or inspiration in complex problem-solving processes to subdivide questions into groups, to structure them to scale and hierarchically, and to relate them to one another. The methodological and ideological influence is undisputed above all in the Anglo-American realm. As a global actor, Jan Gehl underlines the importance of Christopher Alexander in the context of complexity theory in architecture. He calls *A Pattern Language* a work full of suggestions for those studying public life.[10] It is unclear to what extent he picked up ideas and processed them further or who was influenced more by whom, but similarities can be identified in the systematics of urban analyses and method adaptations. This is especially true of his checklist for assessing public space qualities, which has been under constant development since 1974. Nevertheless, while Jan Gehl places people fully in the foreground and subordinates all planning action to them ("first life, then spaces, then buildings"), Christopher Alexander's quest for the proper, living way of building leads to statements that clearly suggest an inverted, distinct space- and form-related viewpoint: *"The life which happens in a building or a town is not merely anchored in the space but made up from the space itself."*[11]

A New Theory of Urban Design,[12] the documentation of a course held in 1978, constitutes a practical urban planning design experiment for a district in San Francisco. It builds upon the experiences of *The Oregon Experiment* (1975) and *A Pattern Language,* and is based on a hierarchy of rules and rule sets with sub-rules for obtaining lively urban structures. The basic hypothesis is that achieving the overarching basic principle of *"Wholeness,"* which has been formulated here for the first time and equated with coherence, can only be accomplished through the process, not just the mere form. The results were subjected to critical self-reflection, with the prospect of being on the right track. Partially serious shortcomings in one's own theory, such as the coordination with existing norms and rules, would, however, have to be overcome first.

---

[9] Jan Gehl, *Life Between Buildings: Using Public Space,* (1971), trans. Jo Koch, New York: Van Nostrand Reinhold, 1987.

[10] Gehl, ibid.

[11] Christopher Alexander, *The Timeless Way of Building,* New York: Oxford University Press, 1979, 74.

[12] Alexander, Neis, Anninou, King: *A New Theory of Urban Design,* New York: Oxford University Press, 1987.

[13] Christopher Alexander, *The Nature of Order: An Essay on the Art of Building and the Nature of the Universe,* (four volumes), Berkeley, CA: The Center for Environmental Structure, 2001–2005.

Christopher Alexander's four-volume opus magnum, *The Nature of Order,*[13] takes up this theme and defines the thoughts more precisely. It is a highly complex system-theoretical work with biological borrowings and philosophical implications for decoding the underlying order of all living structures, and emerged from the realization that patterns, as the key to good building, are not enough. Alexander believes that the deep-seated order that creates life in buildings is a direct result of the physical and mathematical structure of the space, something unambiguous and definitive that can be described and understood, and he attempts to prove this with scientific and empirical methods that are not free of contradictions. The key to good building, therefore, is grounded in the living, three-dimensional order, which must unfold incrementally and in interdependence with positive space from the abstract parameters of "Wholeness" and "Centers," reinforced by fifteen fundamental, concrete properties, and create value in this way. Order derives from a cultural and biological context, and develops buildings and structures from the inside according to a (lost) code inscribed in the human being and the appropriate design vocabulary. "Wholeness" refers to a building or a city in its entirety, but also to the individual parts they are composed of and the relationships of all individual parts to one another. Only when a building, a city, possesses this wholeness, is it beautiful, lively and makes us happy, whereby this wholeness is indivisible, gradually created by a structure-preserving, step-by-step transformation, and unpredictable. All the coherent elements of the whole are called "Centers," which in turn should radiate wholeness for themselves. These centers themselves are lively and support and strengthen each other. Centers are made up of centers. The denser they are, the livelier the whole becomes. With this ordering principle, Christopher Alexander describes self-similarities based on the fractals in nature.

Like his earlier theories, *The Nature of Order* intends to move away from the mechanical planning methods of architecture and their categorizations into right and wrong. Practical tools for this cannot be deduced. In this context, the basic approach itself, namely to reconcile nature, mathematics, scientific principles and feeling through scientific means with the goal to develop objective processes and methods to address subjective emotions, seems to be ambivalent. For example, the juxtaposition of images with the binary answer options of yes or no to the question of the comprised life suggests that there would be a correct answer, as if everyone would see, think and feel the same. And are systematic, objectified design processes not automatically moving into the proximity of engineering and thus in danger of becoming mechanical?

However, the optimistic and humanistic intention to make the built space more vital and human, and thus to come to better, more beautiful cities, remains unfulfilled. Christopher Alexander shares this attitude with the New Urbanism movement, which, at least in the US, largely dominates and implements urban planning discourse. New Urbanism has been established mainly in the United States and Great Britain since the 1990s with precursors such as the "Classicists" Léon and Rob Krier, who, together with Aldo Rossi, were key players in the postmodern uprising. In contrast to the "Classicists", who build urban development projects and use classic design vocabulary, the New Urbanists also offer general principles and rules for urban planning tasks. Basically, like Christopher Alexander, they are formally neutral and propagate building according to timeless values. In detail, however, they are relatively strongly geared to design. Today, there are a variety of different approaches and trends, whereby a new regionalism often forms the basis for the fundamental principles. In a conversation with Michael Mehaffy,[14] Alexander said an alliance with the New Urbanists and the Classicists would be a necessity, because they would sustainably alter the American landscapes. At the same time he criticized the concepts as artificial and—totally in the sense of modernity—the copying of existing set pieces as dishonest.

Co-founded by DPZ – Duany Plater-Zyberk, the CNU[15] (Congress for New Urbanism) even proclaimed its own charter for New Urbanism and today is a movement that has taken hold throughout the United States. Rethinking the American city is the program; the repair of the suburbs and neglected centers are also important fields of action. Mostly, however, new developments are implemented, which also leads to the main criticism that urban sprawl continues, albeit by means of more high-quality neighborhoods and centers.

Andrés Duany names Alexander as one of the most influential figures in the design world, stressing his tremendous influence on Duany's own operational work and that of the CNU environment. The 148 principles of the *Smart Growth Manual* resemble *A Pattern Language*, just like the structure of the *Smart Growth Manual*[16] and other handbooks is based on it. Pattern books have been formulated for various development projects. Duany rejects Alexander's criticism of placing too little attention on the process and genuine participation,

14 ──────────
http://www.katarxis3.com/Alexander.htm [Accessed 06.01.2019].

15 ──────────
http://www.katarxis3.com/Duany.htm [Accessed 06.01.2019].

16 ──────────
Galina Tachieva, *Sprawl Repair Manual,* Washington, DC: Island Press, 2010.

and instead collaborating with commercial project developers as being far from reality. Admittedly, dealing with large scales and leaps in scale is a problem, but also a necessary reality that one must face as well as the market and its forces. Duany calls the hands-on approach and the fine granularity propagated by Alexander a desirable ideal, but considers it romantic to believe that American citizens in their perfect democracy would build the best cities themselves. There is a great need to develop simple programs and tools that help to create good neighborhoods and communities almost automatically and as accurately as possible within the framework of practical needs and the existing bureaucratic system, for example, the smart code as a parametric tool adaptable to local conditions. What appears much more important to him than individually tailored buildings and spaces are adjustable structures that are adaptable in the future, too.

Which closes the circle to some degree. Because even Christopher Alexander said: *"No building is ever perfect."* Each building is approached in a way that it is consistent and good in itself, but reality always proves that we are wrong. It must be constantly further developed.[17] He envisages the step-by-step planning process for this. Duany, as well as Stewart Brand in his book *How Buildings Learn: What Happens After They're Built* (1994), look at the longer-term and interminable reshaping process that makes buildings and the city lively and livable.

The deficits of the urban planning discipline are far from being resolved. The discourse that began in the 1960s appears as current and important today as it was back then. Although the previous gain in knowledge is great, as are the hopes, the right conclusions, nonetheless, have obviously largely still not been drawn. Despite the awareness-building, research, method and process development which has been going on for several generations, the "healing" of the city—to use Alexander's diction—has not yet taken place, in some places not even begun. The instructive findings of the past decades should finally be recognized on a much broader basis than before as a valuable potential to bring them up to date. This definitely includes the legacy of a Christopher Alexander as food for thought. In the dawning Age of the City (since 2008 more than 50 percent of the world's population lives in cities) and after decades of breaches in modernist and postmodern urban planning concepts, it must have slowly become clear that the city cannot be conceived in a monodisciplinary way. Even attempts to understand urbanity and interpret it as a concept

[17] Cf. *The Timeless Way of Building*, 479.

Cf. Andre Krammer, "Von der Allmacht zur Kooperation. Anmerkungen zum Verhältnis von Städtebau(lehre) und Stadtforschung," *dérive* 40/41, Vienna, October–December 2010.

fail without the inclusion of different specialized fields and perspectives. The complexity is far too great for monoperspectives. Just like the activities overlap in space according to Christopher Alexander and relate to each other, it should be the same with the cooperation of the disciplines. Urban planning means theory and practice in the midst of society,[18] which requires a fusion of urban research and urban planning, as well as the involvement of those affected locally. Nobody's professional competence has to be disputed. It is not the end of planning; it is a reorientation, because blurred consensus is not a goal, but rather the best possible outcome from multi-layered perspectives. This is possible in this complex world only through cooperation for the purpose of learning and profiting from each other. But it must also be clear that there will never be a city without fractures, because the fractures belong to the essence of the city and make it what it is.

Christopher Alexander's architectural design and his planning and construction methods are concrete down to the last detail, but urban planning is to only form a framework. Neither in his theories nor in his practical work has Alexander found a satisfactory solution and differentiation for this. Points of contact, however, unquestionably exist. Let us simply start with the honest intention of wanting to do good to the people and our planet.

Norihito Nakatani
Why Recall Christopher Alexander?

from: *10+1 Ten Plus One – Database,* No. 49 (Gendai kenchiku toshi mondōshū 32 | Special issue: Contemporary Architecture 32), Tokyo 2007, 144–145.

A critical re-examination of Christopher Alexander's conceptual framework would undoubtedly be profitable today. Before I devote myself to this task, however, I would like to address the question of how he came to be forgotten.

Christopher Alexander is best known for his theoretical writings *Notes on the Synthesis of Form* (1964)—a logically derived theory of design—and *Pattern Language* (1977). Over the past few years, the publication of *The Nature of Order* has been underway, an overall presentation of his thinking that is to comprise several volumes and more than 2,000 pages.

It is somewhat mystifying that, over the last 20 years, the work of Christopher Alexander has been almost completely forgotten in architectural circles in Japan. Considering the impact his theories of networks have had on other disciplines, most notably computer sciences, where they are considered to be the cornerstone of recent approaches to software engineering, this seems all the more surprising. For Alexander, who originally studied mathematics, architecture—or, to put a finer point to it, the building process—was only one of the many areas he was active in. But it is the idea of "architectural agency," of the "creation of our built environment," that represents the central axis around which his works revolve and in which the synthetic nature underlying his practice is most clearly expressed.

Why, then, has Alexander so seemingly vanished into oblivion? I would claim that one reason for this obliviscence may well be fear—fear that the ruthlessness of Alexander's approach would, in the end, lead to a radical transformation of the architectural profession as such: to the deconstruction not only of existing processes of architectural practice, but also of the positioning of the architect as the focal point in which these processes converge. One may wonder whether what is at play here is indeed oblivion or, rather, an act of repression.

In his first theoretical paper *"The Revolution Finished Twenty Years Ago"* (1960) Alexander argued that the "revolution" of modernist architecture had already sputtered to a halt in the late 1930s, positioning himself literally as a "post-modern" thinker. Somewhat ironically, when the next generation of critics turned its back on postmodernism, decrying it as the "method of historical citation," Alexander's architectural theory came also under fire and was equally discarded.

Taken to its logical conclusion, the approach of diagrammatic architecture and the role it ascribes to diagrams in the architectural process leads us straight back to the obliteration of the subject in Alexander's 1960 paper. By the late 1960s Alexander had already distanced himself from his earlier writings, and, in a surprising turn-around, had begun to formulate an approach that drew its inspiration from patterns underlying natural languages. Accepting the basic tenets of Alexander's theoretical and methodological approach (including his more recent writings) inevitably forces us to adopt a radically altered view not only of the architectural process and the societal interests associated with it, but also of our own positioning within these processes. Who if not us, the post-Alexander generation, would be qualified to open this Pandora's box? We can at least try to retrace the footsteps of his thinking.

In order to do so, I would like to address two issues central to Alexander's theoretical approach:

(1) Design as an Objectively Comprehensible Process

If we take a look at the concept of design outlined in *Notes on the Synthesis of Form* (1964), the process of optimizing physical objects roughly goes as follows: A detailed, comprehensive examination of the individual components that functionally define an existing object (e.g., a kettle) is followed by their reassembly and reunification on the basis of altered parameters. Here, design no longer presents itself as an outflow of the "originality" of an individual, but as an objectively comprehensible process (we are reminded that Rudofsky's *Architecture Without Architects* was published in the very same year).

Alexander's approach attempts to analyze the mysterious process of form finding in mathematical terms: Individual talent or prowess becomes negligible, as the subject's agency in this process is limited to the selection of parameters.

With this, Alexander had opened up his very own Pandora's box. The analysis and synthesis outlined above may still be feasible in the case of a water kettle, but if we apply the same principle to, for instance, the process of designing a building and try to envision and consciously trace every single element or factor involved, we find ourselves confronted with an almost unmanageable flood of variables. It was clear that, at the time, not even the most advanced computer technologies would be able to handle the sheer multitude of actual, existing patterns and factors. For Alexander, under the surface of our everyday understanding and experience of design an overflowing network of forms and relationships lies dormant in the objects themselves. Design, then, is the result of a homeostatic-flexible interplay of "perceived" problems that have come to the fore, and an "intuitive" understanding of harmony—something we can't access through our conscious minds.

(2) The Unconscious in the Architectural Process

It is precisely this unconscious aspect of the design process that guarantees for Alexander the quality of vernacular design vocabularies that have been developed over generations. If we look at the logical development of this idea in Alexander's thinking, it becomes clear that the frequently voiced criticism that what Alexander proposed was merely a simplistic notion of "world harmony" or the populist project of participatory architecture falls short.

In Alexander's writings, we find a sincere reverence for the "harmonious balance" that opens up before our eyes: For him, prior to any conscious human intervention, harmony is already present in the world, embedded not least in our own bodies (conscious intervention may prove obstructive rather than conducive). One cannot stress enough how unusual and radical such an approach is.

The existence of an "unconscious process" can, in and of itself, not possibly be proven or represented on the level of discursive consciousness. We can only resort to an *argumentum ad absurdum* or indirect evidence: How, for example, is it possible for humans to produce poetry—even though they have neither conscious insight into nor control over the process? Freud, too, was forced to fall back on an *argumentum ad absurdum* in order to prove the existence of an elusive unconscious mind.

Alexander's *Pattern Language* was the result of ten years of extensive data collection and empirical verification of this thesis: He set out to subject all aspects of architectural practice, from designing and planning to execution and construction, to a perpetual, open-ended process of testing, questioning and examination—not unlike the stages a writer goes through when writing poetry. It is truly unfortunate that Alexander's own dictum that "anyone can build a house" has so often been misread, and flagrantly misconstrued, as referring to the simple act of cobbling together some wooden beams (it may have been too exhausting for some to read their way through the whole thick book). Even though methodically Alexander's Pattern Language might at first glance appear to be just borrowing from natural language systems, it may actually be better described as an attempt to create an "index"—an index that allows us to identify and grasp the "unconscious processes," and "quality without a name" that underlie, and shape, the process of form finding. Alexander's patterns are not simply a list of principles affecting the construction of spatial structures; for him, human behavior is the crucial element governing the constitution of space. Every pattern is linked to and can be combined with other patterns, just as in an object language subject-predicate-object are always interrelated and acting upon each other.

Who, then, is the "anyone" in "anyone can build a house?" It is most likely something that exists separately from and independently of the conscious subject. What I found so deeply unsettling when

I first encountered Alexander's thinking was precisely the realization that this something also exists within myself.

I am glad to hear that *Notes on the Synthesis of Form*, after years of being out of print, is finally to be reissued.

At the studio of Tezuka Architects, Todoroku, Tokyo, April 2017

"Sometimes inconvenience is luxury."
– A Conversation with Takaharu Tezuka, Tokyo, April 2017

Mr. Tezuka, thank you for the opportunity to have a conversation with you about Christopher Alexander and the Eishin Campus, and about your way of planning and building, which obviously is not foreign to Alexander's ideas. Do you know the Eishin Campus?

I know the Campus, but it has been a long time since I was there. So I cannot say much about how it works today, but I like it; it is great.

What do you especially like about it?

Well, before that, maybe I should explain to you how I think about school buildings, about education: Schools have to be functional, everything has to be safe and functional, and people need to be protected. Everyone thinks of comfort and convenience, but then schools become like IT companies. Every teacher has a small room, all the rooms are connected to each other indoors; nobody gets wet anymore; nobody has to leave the building; everything is comfortable and practical.

But if everything is purposeful and functional, is it really good? Is inconvenience such a bad thing? Isn't inconvenience sometimes a luxury? When you live in the country, you have to take a train, you need a car to go somewhere, you have long ways, but you experience the rain, the wind, the weather. In the city you have the subway, taxis, short ways, you often do not need to leave the protection of the buildings …, but is that really pleasant?

Is that what you want in life?

On a lecture in Dublin about school construction and education before the OECD, I asked the audience what its favorite school building in Dublin was and most of them chose Trinity College, one of the oldest universities in the world—I think older than Oxford. Every time you go to another seminar, you need an umbrella; you have to get out and cross the campus …

Efficiency is not the answer to the desire for well-being and comfort. People do not want and need to be constantly protected.

Here in Japan we drive to the beach in the summer, sometimes it is 50 degrees, and in winter we go skiing at minus 20 degrees—the degree of comfort is therefore not a question of temperature. It is not a question of efficiency. We humans are not machines. And we are not made of sugar.

My family and I like to travel to this particular resort in Indonesia. There is no air conditioning, no covered paths between the individual houses. And if you arrive by plane, you have to rent a car and drive three hours to get there. And then you have to go through the tropical rain to get to the room, for breakfast …

And people love this "inefficiency." It is about experiencing, the direct experience of the weather, of nature. We are misguided—when we plan schools, we are always talking about efficiency. But education is an inefficient industry: Children love to do exactly what they are not allowed to do, and there should be room for that.

Let us return to Alexander. When you were studying, did you get to know Alexander, his theory, the Pattern Language?

Yes, actually I should have brought this book.
Do you have a German copy with you?
I would like to see the difference.

No, the book is too bulky and too heavy to bring here to Japan …

Yes, that is the problem, it is too heavy. I have three copies—an English original and two Japanese editions that I need for my students …

I encountered *A Pattern Language* for the first time during my studies. There was a professor who was quite a big fan of Alexander and introduced us to Chiaki Arai. His architecture is very unlike ours, but he also used Alexander and his theories in many ways and taught them to his students. Arai had studied with Louis Kahn at the University of Pennsylvania.

I was good at making models, but he said, what you do is good building, but that is not architecture; you should go abroad and study there. So I also chose U Penn because they had so many interesting teachers. For example, Mohsen Mostafavi, who wrote a foreword for my *Yellow Book*.

But before I went to the US, I visited the Eishin Campus. At U Penn I learned and understood a lot: for example, that a school is not a building, but a village—that is where I understood Eishin. That is what it was about! Everything else was about functionality and efficiency, but this school was like a small town, designed like a village!

Although we are a modern urban society, we still like to travel to the countryside and walk through a nice, little village. We use all kinds of electronic means, have an iPad and an iPhone, but we have not changed. These electronic tools do not destroy our sense of village. Because, as I said, basically we love inefficiency. Life is not a question of efficiency. Feeling cannot be measured; it is a question of character, personal condition.

I heard all these things in the US; Alexander talked and wrote about them. And later, I also talked to my students at MIT [Musashi Institure of Technology] about it: Why does this tea taste so good? If you ask science, it breaks it down into its individual molecules and explains its ingredients, but it cannot say why it tastes so good. But the explanation is simple: You come in from the cold outside; the hot cup of tea that I put in front of you tastes good because I have always prepared it this way for you and because you now need it to warm yourself up. It is a kind of instinct ... It is about this balance. The truth is, and that is what Christopher Alexander believes, it goes beyond pure existence; it is about the in-between, the balance. The answer is not in a single object, it is about the whole thing.

There is also this sentence by Peter Cook, whom my wife was a student of: The observation is far more important than the analysis. We have focused too much on the analysis and have watched too little! If you observe, then you have to step back, you have to feel what is going on.

When you were studying, the Campus was not quite finished—apart from the fact that certain parts have not been realized until today.

I studied in Tokyo in the mid-1980s and visited the Campus before moving to the US. It wasn't finished. The ground was quite muddy I remember.

That is probably still the case today, in the rain and snow. – When studying your own projects such as the Sora no Mori Clinic or the Child Chemo House, there are many parallels to the Campus facility—not only the human scale, but also the layout and positioning of the buildings, the paths between the pavilions ...

I do not make references; I do not look at his books to design. Alexander and the Pattern Language give me a base.

It is like having a language: Once you have learned it, you do not read in the grammar book anymore. It is the same with me. *A Pattern Language* forms the basis which I build upon. I did not understand everything here in Tokyo, as I said, but when I studied at U Penn, where the legacy of Louis Kahn prevailed, I had Mohsen Mostafavi—you know that he worked together

Sketch for Sora no Mori Clinic, Architects Catalogue 3, Work number 93 with Rem Koolhaas at the Venice Biennale—a teacher who talked about autonomy and context. So before we started class with him, we had to get acquainted with Alexander, but it took a long time to understand what he was saying.

And the Child Chemo House or the Sora na Mori Clinic is not about reference, it is about a kind of unconscious control. Alexander gave me a base, a grammar.

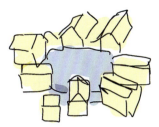

Sketch for Child Chemo House, *Architects Catalogue 3*, Work number 85

In various conversations here in Tokyo we have gained the impression that Alexander is perceived as a very ambivalent personality ...

In what sense do you mean "ambivalent?"

Well, he is a difficult, controversial person; he has great ideas, but he is difficult when it comes to implementing and asserting these ideas.

Yes, he is difficult, that is right.

We were told that he was very popular at first and not least because the Eishin Campus was well-known and well-received, but after completion it was no longer like that. There were difficulties and sometimes he was even rejected.

But that is the way people are, they like to complain about this and that; the neighbors had objections ... but the majority here in Japan still appreciates him and he is not forgotten.

The fact that he is widely known in Japan—Was this due to his contribution to the Japanese Pavilion at the Osaka EXPO 1970, or first through the Eishin Campus or through the early translations of his books?

In my student days here in Tokyo probably only two people read *A Pattern Language*. It was exciting, but also very difficult to understand.

At the Eishin Campus, Alexander attempted to shift the patterns into the cultural context of Japan, as he described in his book The Battle for the Life and Beauty of the Earth.

Well, he did not just copy the Japanese style; he tried to bring in Western style.

What do you think about this "shifting of patterns," about this attempt to transfer something into the Japanese culture?

In order to talk about these things, we really need to talk about what Japanese culture is. There are so many nationalists saying we are pure Japanese, we have a great, traditional Japanese culture! But that is not true. In fact, it is a fusion, a mixture. You know we have the oldest timber buildings in the world, but those who came here to build them stayed and became Japanese. It is a real Japanese building, but it came from elsewhere. And there are so many Koreans and Chinese here, and all became Japanese.

    Japan is the end of the world—you know the story of Marco Polo, who was looking for gold—and at that time we were producing the largest amount of gold in the world. It was hard to get to Japan. Japanese culture is a hybrid of many cultures, with influences from the Koreans, the Chinese, the British, the Germans and the Dutch. My family was also trading with the East India Company—we imported Art Nouveau to Japan.

So what Christopher Alexander did is okay, but there is one thing I am concerned about: He only imported the old part of Europe. He could have imported the latest, newest part!

For example, the school I am teaching at was built by a pupil of Walter Gropius. He imported modern style—but 50 years after studying with Gropius.

And what Alexander does is even older. But the important idea behind it that I have learned is that it is not about style issues, it is about something beyond it. He tried to teach us timelessness! He wanted to design the timeless. The good sides of Alexander's architecture lie in the timelessness.

Takaharu + Yui Tezuka:
Architecture Catalogue, 3 volumes, Japanese/English, Tokyo: TOTO Publishing, 2006, 2009, 2015

You picked up on this term in the documentation of your work—you titled the epilogue to the first volume "Time-less."

Yes, the point is that regardless of periods and fashions, there are architectural elements that do not change. And the relationship between people and architecture does not change. Alexander's eclecticism may not work very well here and there, and is somehow outdated, but the Tokyo Station—its builder was a then-famous modern architect, Tatsuno Kingo—is an eclectic building and is outdated today, but it works wonderfully.

In that sense, I think Alexander's way of designing is okay, because there is so much timelessness;

Tokyo Station

the buildings are far better than most new, modern buildings in Japan.

Emoto Apartment Building, Honkomagome, Tokyo

Do you know the Emoto Apartment Building here in Tokyo in Honkomagome? It was realized by Alexander and his team in 1989.

I know about it, but I have never been there.

It is a multi-unit house in a mansion district, which fits in there very well and is first not noticeable at all, but in detail one sees very many typical Alexander patterns. – But again to your texts: In 2009 you had an exhibition in Frankfurt at the German Architecture Museum DAM entitled Nostalgic Future – Remembered Future. How do you interpret the word "nostalgic?"

That is a dangerous word. People dream of the Middle Ages, but they have no idea how it was to live back then; that it was perhaps even more brutal than today's IS. There were epidemics and witch burnings and slavery ... You have illusions about a particular lifestyle, but what is the nature of these illusions?

Basically, it is all about the longing for touch, for warmth, away from cold technology and machines. We built the Sora no Mori Clinic in wood. The timber construction is not only an old technology, but can also be very modern—that is what we call "nostalgic future." The future always comes in the form of technology—think of the films *Modern Times* or *Tron* or *The Matrix*. We have to digest the meaning of the past; it is more an idealism than a nostalgia. Christopher Alexander can serve here as a role model with his kind of romanticism.

Is Alexander's method of designing and planning relevant for today's and future construction tasks? If not so much for the big ones, then for the smaller ones?

A Pattern Language is a kind of Bible. There are many ways to interpret it. If you read the Bible today, you find that it is very brutal, but it is a very long story with many interpretations.

Alexander gave us his "Bible" as a basis and we can build on that. So it is not about copying—that is how it works, that is how *A Pattern Language* should be understood.

Hajo Neis, Ingrid King, Christopher Alexander, 1982

Biography Christopher Alexander

Christopher Alexander, born on October 4, 1936 in Vienna, spent the first years of his life in Vienna-Döbling, on Krottenbachstraße, resp., Goltzgasse. In 1939, the family had to emigrate to England, where his father, Ferdinand Johann Alexander, a university-trained archaeologist like his wife, found work again as a secondary school teacher. Alexander grew up in Oxford and Chichester, studied mathematics (MA) and architecture (BArch) at Cambridge, and completed his architecture studies at Harvard University with a dissertation (PhD) entitled *Notes on the Synthesis of Form*, for which he received the first and only gold medal for research from the AIA – American Institute of Architects. In 1963, he was appointed as a professor at the University of California, Berkeley and, in 1967, founded the Center for Environmental Structure at 2701 Shasta Road, Berkeley, which he headed until his retirement in 2001. He established the web platform patternlanguage.com in 2000. Alexander and his first wife Pamela have two daughters, Lily and Sophie. In 2002, he moved with his second wife, Maggie Moore Alexander, to England, where he lives in Meadow Lodge, West Sussex, as an advisor and consultant.

Prizes and Awards (Selection)

1972   First Gold Medal for Research by the American Institute of Architects
1986   ACSA Distinguished Professor Award
1994   Seaside Prize
1996   Fellow of the American Academy of Arts and Sciences
2006   Athena Award
2009   Vincent Scully Prize
2011   Lifetime Achievement Award by the Urban Design Group

Buildings and Projects by Christopher Alexander and CES (Selection)

1962   Village school, Bavra, Gujarat, India (with Janet Johnson)
1962   Master plan for Bavra, Gujarat, India
1964   Schematic design of stations for the Bay Area Rapid Transit (BART), San Francisco, CA (with Maren van King, Sara Ishikawa)
1969   Master plan for the University of Oregon, Eugene, OR
1969   Design for 1,500 low-cost houses, Lima, Peru — invited competition entry for the UN, 1st prize (with Sara Ishikawa, Sanford Hirshen, etc.)
1970   81 exhibition panels for Osaka EXPO, Japanese Pavilion "A Human City" (with Ronald Walkey and others)
1971   14 prototypical low-cost houses, Lima, Peru (with Sara Ishikawa and others)
1972   Development of a master plan for Marsta, Sweden (with Max Jacobson, Ingrid King)
1972   County Mental Health Center, Modesto, CA (with Murray Silverstein and others)
1974   Etna Street Cottage experimental house project (featherweight construction) (with Walter Wendler and others)
1974   User-designed apartment building (27 families), schematic design and construction schedule, Paris (with Ingrid King, Walter Wendler)
1976   Mexicali Project (low-cost residential and working district), Mexicali, Mexico
1978–1980. Martinez Workshop (experimental concrete structures), Martinez, CA
1980   The Linz Café (wooden building incl. furnishings in the scope of the Forum Design exhibition), Linz, Austria
1981   Master plan for Guasare New Town, Maracaibo, Venezuela
1981   Master plan for the community of North Omaha, Omaha, NE
1981–1985. Eishin Campus (29 buildings and garden design) in Iruma-shi near Tokyo, Saitama Prefecture, Japan (with Hajo Neis, project architect, Gary Black, Ingrid King, and others)
1982   Terraced house on four levels, with seven buildings, Lake Berryessa, CA, for John and Mara Lighty
1982   Sapporo Apartment Buiulding, shops, 43 families, Sapporo, Japan (with Ingrid King)
1982   Comprehensive master plan pattern language for the University of Missouri, Kansas City, MO
1983   Sala House, Albany, CA
1983   Master plan, design of 30 houses, kindergarten, etc., Galilee, Israel
1983   Fresno Farmers Market, Fresno, CA (with Carl Lindberg, Jonathan Fefferman)
1984–1985. Neighborhood plan for 150 low-cost houses, São Carlos, Brazil
1985   Heavy timber carpentry workshop, Martinez, CA (with Gary Black)
1985–1987. Seminar buildings on Eishin Campus, Iruma-shi, Japan
1988   Potash-McCabe House, San Anselmo, CA
1988   Second Sala House, Albany, CA
1988   Medlock-Graham House, Whidbey Island, Seattle, WA
1988   Master plan and building plans for Pasadena Waldorf School, Altadena, CA
1988   King House, Snowmass, CO
1988   Emoto Apartment Building, Tokyo, Japan (with Hajo Neis)
1989   Exemplary ecological planning of 60 houses, Mendham Township, NJ
1990   Exhibition Galleries, De Young Museum, San Francisco, CA
1990   Lighty House, Berryessa, CA
1990   Julian Street Inn, Shelter for the Homeless, San Jose, CA (with Gary Black, Elene Coromvli)
1990–1991. Shiratori Plan, low-rise, high-density settlement for 500 families, Nagoya, Japan
1991   Kaiser-Anderton House, Palo Alto, CA
1991–1993. Student housing for the University of Oregon (300 units), Eugene, OR
1991   The Mary Rose Museum (project commissioned by the Prince of Wales), Portsmouth, England
1991–1993. Agate Street Dormitory for student families, for University of Oregon, Eugene, OR
1992   Chikusadai-Plan, hochverdichtete Siedlung für 800 Familien, Hazama und Kusunoki, Nagoya, Japan
1992   Upham House, Berkeley, CA
1992   Sullivan House, Berkeley, CA
1994–1995. Back of the Moon Community, three private homes, Lake Travis, TX
1994–1996. West Dean College Gardens Visitor Center, West Sussex, England
2002   Clubhouse on Eishin Campus, Iruma-Shi, Japan (with Randy Schmidt, Masaya Okada, Miyoko Tsutsui)

Book Publications by Christopher Alexander

Christopher Alexander, Hansjoachim Neis and Maggie Moore Alexander, *The Battle for the Life and Beauty of the Earth. A Struggle Between Two World-Systems*, New York: Oxford University Press, 2012

The Nature of Order – Vol. 1, *The Phenomenon of Life* (2001); vol. 2, *The Process of Creating Life* (2002); vol. 3, *A Vision of a Living World* (2005); vol. 4, *The Luminous Ground* (2004), Berkeley, CA: Center for Environmental Structure, [New York: Oxford University Press]

(with Gary Black and Miyoko Tsutsui), *The Mary Rose Museum*, New York: Oxford University Press, 1995

A Foreshadowing of 21st Century Art: The Color and Geometry of Very Early Turkish Carpets, New York: Oxford University Press, 1993 (with Hajo Neis, Artemis Anninou and Ingrid King), *A New Theory of Urban Design,* New York: Oxford University Press, 1987 [trans. Jap. 1989]

(with Howard Davis, Julio Martinez and Donald Corner): *The Production of Houses,* New York: Oxford University Press, 1985

The Linz Café / Das Linz Café, New York and Vienna: Oxford University Press/Löcker Verlag, 1981 [Eng./Ger.]

(with Howard Davis), *Rebirth of the Inner City. The North Omaha Plan,* Berkeley, CA: Center for Environmental Structure, 1981

The Timeless Way of Building, New York: Oxford University Press, 1979 [trans. Span. 1981]

(with Sara Ishikawa, Murray Silverstein, Max Jacobson, Ingrid Fiksdahl-King and Shlomo Angel), *A Pattern Language: Towns Buildings Construction,* New York: Oxford University Press, 1977 [trans. Span. 1980; Dutch 1982; Jap. 1984; Ger. 1995]

(with Sara Ishikawa and Murray Silverstein), *The Oregon Experiment,* New York: Oxford University Press, 1975 [trans. Fr. 1976; Jap. 1977; Ital. 1977; Span. 1980]

(with Howard Davis and Halim Abdelhalim), *People Rebuilding Berkeley. The Self-Creating Life of Neighborhoods,* CES, Berkeley, CA: Center for Environmental Structure, 1975. Reprint by New Communities Development Group, Berkeley, CA, 1985

La estructura del medio ambiente, Barcelona: Tusquets Editores, 1971

(with Ronald Walkey, Murray Silverstein et al.), *A Human City,* Tokyo: Kajima Publishing Company, 1970

(with Sanford Hirshen, Sara Ishikawa, Christie Coffin and Shlomo Angel), *Houses Generated by Patterns,* Berkeley, CA; Center for Environmental Structure, 1969

Tres aspectos de matematica y diseño, Barcelona: Tusquets Editores, 1969

(with Sara Ishikawa, Murray Silverstein and the Center for Environmental Structure), *A Pattern Language Which Generates Multi-Service Centers,* Berkeley, CA: Center for Environmental Structure, 1968

The City as a Mechanism for Sustaining Human Contact, Berkeley, CA: Center for Planning and Development Research, University of California, 1966

(with Barry Poyner), *The Atoms of Environmental,* Center for Planning and Development Research, Berkeley, CA: University of California, Berkeley, 1966

Notes on the Synthesis of Form, Cambridge, MA: Harvard University Press, 1964 [trans. Ital. 1967; Span. 1969; Fr. 1971]

(with Serge Chermayeff), *Community and Privacy. Toward a New Architecture of Humanism,* Garden City, NY: Doubleday, 1963 [trans. Ital. 1965; Jap. 1966; Span. 1967; Ger. 1970]

Articles by Christopher Alexander in Magazines and Books (Selection)

"Regelbasiertes Entwerfen: Pattern, Diagramm, Archetyp. Von fließender Systematik und generativen Prozessen. Christopher Alexander im Gespräch mit Rem Koolhaas und Hans Ulrich Obrist," ARCH+ 189, October 2008, 20–25

"The Generative Urban Code," *New Urbanism and Beyond. Designing Cities for the Future,* edited by Tigran Haas, New York: Rizzoli, 2008

"Sustainability and Morphogenesis: The Rebirth of a Living World," *Structurist,* 2007–08, 47–48, 12–19

"An Interview with Christopher Alexander," *Structurist,* 2005–06, 45–46, 4–21

"The Nature of Alexander" (interview), *Clem Labine's Traditional Building,* 2005, 5, vol. 18, 12–15

"Our New Architecture and the Many World Cultures," *Clem Labine's Traditional Building,* 2005, 1, vol. 18, 210

"Alexander Centering," *Architecture Week* 249, 2005

"Interacting with Christopher Alexander" (interview), *Architecture & Design* 3, 2002, vol. 19, 93–97

"Perspectives: Manifesto 1991," *Progressive Architecture,* July 1991, 108–112

Interview with Christopher Alexander, *Architecture & Design,* 1, 1991, vol. 8, 93–99

"Low-Rise High-Density Housing in Nagoya," *Asahi Shimbun,* March 23, 1990

(with Hajo Neis, Ingrid King, Artemis Anninou and Gary Black), "Mountain View Civic Center Competition Design," *a+u* 228, September 1989, 21–46

"Architecture Operating within a World View," *Complexities of the Human Environment: A Cultural and Technological Perspective* (= Proceedings from the Discoveries 1987 Symposium), edited by Karl Vak, Vienna: Europa Verlag, 1988, 129–133

"The End of Post-Modernism," *Concrete,* Spring 1988, 3, vol. 25, 23–25

"The Style of the Twenty-First Century: An Essay on Technology, Geometry and Style," *Precis 6,* The Journal of the Columbia University Graduate School of Architecture, Planning and Preservation, 1987, 128–137

(with Hajo Neis), "Great Hall + Homebase Street. Eishin Gakuen Higashino Koko," Kankyou Kouzou Center (CES), *Shin Kenchiku. The Japan Architect,* 7, 1987, 118–119

(with Artemis Anninou, Gary Black and John Rheinfrank), "Toward a Personal Workplace," *Architectural Record,* 11, 1987, vol. 175, 130–141

Introduction to "Das Machen von Gebäuden: Eishin College – Eishin High School bei Tokio," *Baumeister* 83, 2, 1986, 24 (with Hajo Neis, Gary Black and Ingrid King), "Battle: The History of a Crucial Clash between World-System A and World-System B – Construction of the New Eishin Campus," *Shin Kenchiku. The Japan Architect,* 8, 1985, 8, 15–35

"Sketches of a New Architecture," *Architecture in an Age of Skepticism,* edited by Denys Lasdun, London: Architectural Press, 1984, 8–27

"Mexicali Revisited," *Places,* vol. 1, Summer 1984, Cambridge, MA: The MIT Press, 4, 76–77

(with Barry Poyner), "The Atoms of Environmental Structure," *Developments in Design Methodology,* edited by Nigel Cross, Chichester: John Wiley and Sons, 1984, 123–133

"Eine Pattern Language – Auszüge aus 'Die zeitlose Art zu Bauen' und 'Eine Pattern Language'," *ARCH+* 73, March 1984, 14–37

"Zur Macht der Gefühle. Peter Eisenman im Gespräch mit Christopher Alexander," *ARCH+* 73, March 1984, 70–73

"Discord Over Harmony in Architecture: The Eisenman/Alexander Debate," *HGSD News,* May–June 1983, 5, vol. 11, 12–17 (trans. Jap. 1984, Ger. 1984)

"Notes on Pattern Language in the Office," *Office Furniture,* vol. II of ALBUM, edited by Mario Bellini, 1983, 97–101

(with Artemis Anninou and Hansjoachim Neis), "Wholeness in the Structure of the City," 124–129; "The San Francisco Waterfront Project," *Architecture in Greece,* 11982, 16, 159–167

Interview with Howard Davis, "Beyond Humanism," *Journal of Architectural Education,* vol. 35, Fall 1981, 1, 18–24

"Kunst und Design für das 21. Jahrhundert," 101–114; "Der Fortschritt meiner Arbeit 1958–1980," 385–394; "Anmerkungen zum Design des Linz-Café," 664–667, *Design ist unsichtbar,* edited by Helmut Gsöllpointer, Angela Hareiter and Laurids Ortner, Vienna: Löcker Verlag, 1980

"The Linz Cafe," *Architectural Design,* March/April 1980, 48–49

"The Architect Builder: Toward Changing the Conception of What an Architect Is," *San Francisco Bay Architect's Review,* September 1977, 4, 4

(with Halim Abdelhalim, Walter Wendler et al.), "Tourism in Andalusia: Making Buildings and Communities which Really Live," *Architectural Design,* January 1975, 1, vol. 45, 33–37

"Timeless Way of Building," *a+u* 51, March 1975, 49–60

(with Sara Ishikawa and Murray Silverstein), "A Collection of Patterns which Generate Multi-Service Centers," edited by Declan und Margrit Kennedy, *Architects' Year Book – The Inner City,* vol. 14, London 1974, 141–180

Interview with Maria Luisa Racionero, *Funcion de la Arquitectura Moderna,* Barcelona: Salvat Editores, 1973, 8–21 and 64–73

"An Attempt to Derive the Nature of a Human Building System from First Principles," 22–32; Interview with Max Jacobson: "The Invention of a Human and Organic Building System," 33–51, *Shirt-Sleeve Session on Responsive Housebuilding Technologies,* edited by Edward Allen, Cambridge, MA: The MIT Press, 1972

"Houses Generated by Patterns," *Architects' Year Book 13,* 1971, 84–114

"Changes in Form," *Architectural Design,* 1970, vol. 40, 122–125

"System Denken – Moderne Version des Gefühls für Wunder," *Baumeister,* December 1969, vol. 65, 1452–1459

"The Bead Game Conjecture," *Lotus 5,* 1968, Venice: Editoriale Lotus, 151–154

"The Environmental Pattern Language," *Ekistics,* May 1968, vol. 25, 336–337

"Major Changes in Environmental Form Required by Social and Psychological Demands," Second International Seminar, Japan Center for Area Development Research, September 1968, 66–83 (last reprinted in *Struktur Frihed Form,* edited by Peter Broberg and Karen Zahle, Copenhagen: Arkitektens Forlag,1976, 77–95)

"Design Innovation. An Exchange of Ideas," *Progressive Architecture,* 11, 1967, vol. 48, 126–131

"Die Stadt ist kein Baum," *Bauen + Wohnen* 21, 7,1967, 283–290

"Systems Generating Systems," *Systemat,* Journal of the Inland Steel Products Company, 1967 (last reprinted in *Computational Design Thinking,* edited by Achim Menges und Sean Ahlquist, Chichester: John Wiley & Sons, 2011, 58–67)

"From a Set of Forces to a Form," *The Man-Made Object. Vision and Value Series,* vol. 4, edited by György Kepes, New York: George Braziller, 1966, 96–107

"The Pattern of Streets," *Journal of the AIP,* September 1966, 3, vol. 32, 273–278

"Twenty-Six Entrance Relations for a Suburban House," *The Atoms of Environmental Structure,* Ministry of Public Buildings and Works, Directorate of Research and Development, London: Ministry of Public Buildings and Works, 1966, 17–7

"Relational Complexes in Architecture," *Architectural Record,* 3, 1966, vol. 140, 185–190

"The Coordination of the Urban Rule System," *Regio Basiliensis Proceedings,* Basel, 12, 1965, 1–9

"A City is Not a Tree," *Architectural Forum,* 2, 1965, vol. 122, 58–62 [trans., among others, Ger. 1967]

"The Theory and Invention of Form," *Architectural Record,* 4, 1 1965, vol. 137, 177–186

"A Much Asked Question about Computers and Design," *Architecture and Computers,* Boston: Boston Architectural Center, 1964, 52

"The Most Stable Decomposition of a System into Subsystems," *Information and Control,* 1963

"Hidecs 3: Four Computer Programs for the Hierarchical Decomposition of Systems which Have an Associated Linear Graph," *Civil Engineering Systems Laboratory Publication Report R63–27,* Cambridge MA: MIT School of Engineering, 1963, 6

"Twenty-six Pictures to the Top of the Tree," *Architectural Forum,* October 1963

(with A. W. F. Huggins), "On Changing the Way People See," *Perceptual and Motor Skills,* 19, 1, July 1964, 235–253

"The Determination of Components for an Indian Village," *Proceedings of the Conference on Design Method,* London, September 1963, Oxford: Pergamon Press, 1963

(with Marvin Manheim): "Hidecs 2: A Computer Program for the Hierarchical Decomposition of a Set with an Associated Graph," *Civil Engineering Systems Laboratory Publication Report R62-2,* Cambridge, MA: MIT School of Engineering, 1968

"The Origin of Creative Power in Children," *British Journal of Aesthetics,* vol. 3, 2, July 1962, 207–226

"Information and an Organized Process of Design," *Proceedings of the BRT,* Washington, Spring 1961, 115–124

"The Revolution Finished Twenty Years Ago," *Architects' Year Book,* vol. 9, London 1960, 181–185

"Perception and Modular Coordination," *RIBA Journal,* 12, October 1959, vol. 66, 425–429

Websites (Selection)

www.patternlanguage.com
www.livingneighborhoods.org
www.katarxis3.com
https://ced.berkeley.edu/ced/faculty-staff/christopher-alexander
www.librarything.com/series/Center+for+Environmental+Structure+Series
http://eishin.ac

Secondary Literature about Christopher Alexander / Eishin Campus (Selection)

Czech, Hermann, "Christopher Alexander and Viennese Modernism," in Hermann Czech, *Essays on Architecture and City Planning,* Zurich: Park Books, 2019

Namba, Kazuhiku and Kitayama, Kō, "Daiarōgu: Patan rangēji wa sūkōsa ni tōtatsu dekiru ka [Conversation: Which Degree of Abstraction Can the Pattern Language Reach?]," Yokohama Graduate School of Architecture (ed.), *Nijūsseki no shisō kara kangaeru, korekara no toshi kenchiku* [Theoreticians of the 20th Century: City and Architecture of the Future], Tokyo: Shōkokusha, 2016, 183–194

Mead, Derrick, "Christopher Alexander," *Metropolis,* January 2012, 6, vol. 31, 55

Nakatani, Norihito, *Severarunesu plus: Jibutsu rensa to toshi kenchiku ningen / Severalness+: City, Architecture and Human Beings as the Cycle of Things),* Tokyo: Kajima Shuppankai, 2011

Kühn, Christian, "Christopher Alexanders Pattern Language," *ARCH+* 189, October 2008, 26–31

Nakatani, Norihito, "Areguzanda ga saishōkan sarete imasu ga, naze desu ka? [Why Christopher Alexander Is Experiencing a Revival]," *10+1,* 49, 2007, 144–145

Mehaffy, Michael, "Notes on the Genesis of Wholes. Christopher Alexander and His Continuing Influence," *Urban Design International,* 1, 2007, vol. 12, 41–57

Leitner, Helmut, *Mustertheorie – Einführung und Perspektiven auf den Spuren von Christopher Alexander,* Graz: Nausner & Nausner, 2007

Portugali, Nili, *Entwurfsprozess und Genius loci. Eine ganzheitlich phänomenologische Annäherung an Architektur,* Fellbach: Edition Axel Menges, 2006

Davis, Howard, "Four Reviews and an Overview of Christopher Alexander's 'The Nature of Order,'" *Structurist,* 2005–06, 45–46, 22–47

Salingaros, Nikos A., "The Structure of Pattern Languages," *Architectural Research Quarterly,* 2, 2000, vol. 4, 149–161

Kühn, Christian, "Diagrams Are Forever: Christopher Alexander's 'Pattern Language' and 'Notes on the Synthesis of Form,'" *Daidalos,* Dec. 1998–Jan. 1999, 69–70, 136–145

Kühn, Christian, "Maschinelle (Ir)rationalität: Computer Aided Design, Konvention und die Genese von Form," *Archithese* 1, 1998, vol. 28, 22–27

Nute, Kevin, "Cambridge Patterns at Christopher Alexander's Eishin School," *a+u* 95:08, 4–7

Karatani, Kojin, *Architecture as Metaphor: Language, Number, Money,* with an introduction by Arata Isozaki, "A Map of Crises," Cambridge, MA, The MIT Press, 1995

Ganser, Renate and Schrom, Georg, "Der Mond ist unter. Geblieben: Die vier Ecken des Tisches. Christopher Alexander im Gespräch mit Georg Schrom," *Architektur aktuell,* July/August 1995, 92–101

King, Ingrid F., "Christopher Alexander and Contemporary Architecture," *Special Issue of a+u* 93:08

Ando, Misako, "Conversation with an American Architect, Mr. Christopher Alexander: 'High-Rise for Lack of Land' Is Wrong, It Is Possible to Create High-Density Human Living Environment with Low-Rise Houses," *Mainichi Newspaper,* Tokyo, March 24, 1991

"Armonía y totalidad: En el campus de New Eishin," *CA: Revista Oficial del Colegio de Arquitectos de Chile,* 1991, 63, 39–41

Shibusawa, Kazuhiko, "To Houses with Own Garden from High-Rise Houses: A Proposal by Mr. Christopher Alexander," *Sankei,* March 14, 1991, 19

Entries In The International Architectural Design Competition For The Tokyo International Forum, 1989, Japan Institute of Architects, March 26, 1990 (Christopher Alexander, 133)

Matsuba, Kazukiyo, "Komagome Building," *Box,* April 1989, 12–15

Ichikawa, Hiroshi, "In Pursuit of the Possibility of 'Place' – School Architecture of Christopher Alexander," *Search for Self and Search for the Cosmos,* Tokyo: Iwanami Shoten, March 1989, 147–168

"Eishin School, Higashino High School," *Inax Booklet,* 2, 1988, vol. 8, 25–28

"Maison de Louran (Emoto Building)," *Nikkei Architecture,* 6–13, 1988, 62–69

"Eishin School," *Nikkei Architecture,* 7–27, 1987, 148–156

Matsui, Gengo, *Fringes: A Visual Approach to the Understanding of Structures,* Tokyo: Kajima Institute Publishing Co., 1986, 48–59

Neis, Hansjoachim, "Fundamental Conditions Necessary for the Creation of Green Space in a City," *International Green Forum Report,* September 1986, 111–113

Peters, Paulhans, "'Pattern' und 'Postmodern'," *Baumeister* 83, 2, 1986, 6

Neis, Hansjoachim, "Das Machen von Gebäuden: Eishin College, Eishin High School bei Tokio," *Baumeister* 83, 2, 1986, 24–42

Viladas, P. and Fisher, T., "Harmony and Wholeness: Christopher Alexander," *Progressive Architecture,* 1986, 67(6), 92–103

Banham, Reyner, "Wechselnde Richtungen auf dem zeitlosen Weg," *ARCH+* 86, 1986, 12–14

Kostulski, Thomas, "Eine Schule als Dorf: Eishin Schule, Tokio: Center for Environmental Structure; Christopher Alexander," *ARCH+* 81, 8, 1985, 66–69

"Eishin-gakuen Higashino Senior High School by Christopher Alexander and C.E.S.," *Kenchiku Bunka,* 1985, 6, vol. 40, 27–60

Ide, Takashi, Namba, Kazuhiko, Higuchi, Hiroyasu and Funo Shūji, "Teoi no yutopia. Higashino-kōkō ni nani ga mieta ka? [The Injured Utopia. What Does the Higashino High School Project Show Us?]," *Kenchiku Bunka,* 1985, 6/2, 28–54

Matsuba, Kazukiyo, "Kindai to no arasoi [Struggle with Modernism]," *Shin Kenchiku. The Japan Architect,* 6, 1985, 153–164

"The Battle of the Building Systems," *Architect & Builder,* 1985, 28–29

Neis, Hajo, "The Building Process – Eishin Campus," *Nikkei Architecture,* 5–20, 1985, 58–68

[Eishin], *Toshi-Jutaku,* May 1985, 5–46

Namba, Kazuhiko, "Pattern Language as a Man-Architecture System," *a+u* 183, 12, 1985, 4–5

"Christopher Alexander," *ARCH+* 73, March 1984 (Special Issue)

Kuhnert, Nikolaus, "Editorial," *ARCH+* 73, 13–14

Davis, Howard, "Moshav Shorashim," *ARCH+* 73, 44–45

Petermann, Ken, "Eishin Schule, Tokyo," *ARCH+* 73, 48–52

Siepl, Susanne, "Neues aus Berkeley – mein Studium bei Christopher Alexander," *ARCH+* 73, 54–57

Vargas, Eduardo, "...Lehre gesprochen," *ARCH+* 73, 58–59

Eith, Ludwig, Marlow, Kay and Maurer, Andreas, "Rolfshagen – Erfahrungen mit der Pattern Language aus der Sicht der Bewohner und Planer," *ARCH+* 73, 60–62

Czech, Hermann, "Christopher Alexander und die Wiener Moderne," *ARCH+* 73, 63–65

Kovatsch, Manfred A., "...von Mustern, die einen gewöhnlichen Ort lebenswert machen," *ARCH+* 73, 65–69

Nakano, Hiroshi, "Seeking For a New Paradigm: Logic and Practice of Christopher Alexander," *Axis,* January 1983, vol. 6, 30–35

Peterman, Ken: *The Eishin School Project,* Master's Thesis, University of California, Berkeley, CA, May 1983

Grabow, Stephen, *Christopher Alexander – The Search for a New Paradigm in Architecture*, London–Boston: Oriel Press (Routledge and Kegan Paul, PLC), 1983

Habermas, Jürgen, "Moderne und postmoderne Architektur", *ARCH+* 61, February 1982, 54–59

Pe[ters, Paulhans], "Das 'Linz Café'. Anläßlich der Ausstellung 'Forum Design' in Linz/Donau," *Baumeister* 4, 1982, 329–333

Kovatsch, Manfred, "Notizen zu Christopher Alexanders 'Pattern Language'," *UM BAU* 5, December 1981, 5–17

Cook, Peter, "Forum Design. Preview of exhibition, Linz, Austria," *Architectural Design,* 1980, 3–4, vol. 50, 42–66

Clavan, Benjamin, "Christopher Alexander and The Pattern Language: From Theory to Reality," *a+u,* December 1979, 87–98

Hirata, K., "Christopher Alexander's Timeless Way of Building," *a+u* 5, 3.1975, 49–60

"Alexander," *Toshi-Jutaku,* appearing in successive issues from September to December 1970, Nos. 29–32

Nitschke, Gunter, "Theory of Environmental Design, Complexity VI," *Toshi-Jutaku,* June 1969, 14, 94–96

Sugiyama, Fumimasa, *Christopher Alexander on Design Process,* Graduation Thesis from the Tokyo Institute of Technology, December 1969

Asada, Takashi, "Review of Christopher Alexander's Writings," *Approach,* Spring 1968, 22–27

Author Biographies

Ernst Beneder (Vienna) b. 1958; Architect Dipl.Ing. in Vienna since 1987, architecture office with Anja Fischer; 1984 and 1988/89 Postgraduate Studies at the Tokyo Institute of Technology, Fellow of the Japan Society for the Promotion of Science. Visiting professorships and teaching at the Vienna University of Technology, the University of Illinois, the École Nationale Supérieure d'Architecture de Versailles, the Universidad Técnica Federico Santa María in Valparaíso, Chile, the Tokyo University of Science and the University of Stuttgart. Worked on design advisory boards (Feldkirch, Krems, Steyr, Eisenstadt, Wels, Wörgl, Innsbruck, Graz and Salzburg), in numerous juries (most recently for the renovation of the Austrian Parliament Building in Vienna) and architectural institutions (ORTE architekturnetzwerk NÖ, ÖGFA – Austrian Society for Architecture, Architecture Advisory Council of the Austrian Federal Real Estate Company [BIG]). Completed projects (selection): Tower Extension S, Haus Ausee IV, Waidhofen/Ybbs Town Hall, Neurological Center of the Otto Wagner Spital in Vienna-Hietzing, Sparkasse Lower Austria headquarters in St. Pölten, parish churches in Gallspach, Lingenau, Dornbirn Oberdorf and Weidling, and the Protestant church in Mitterbach. Urban development projects: The City Project in Waidhofen/Ybbs, The SteyrPlan, Advanced Information City Kawasaki. Awards, among others: Otto Wagner Urban Architecture Award, Pilgram Preis, Culture Awards of the State of Lower Austria and the City of Waidhofen/Ybbs, Central Glass (Tokyo), Urban Renewal Award of the City of Vienna.

Eva Guttmann (Graz/Vienna) b. 1967; studied political science, history and architecture (Mag. Dipl. Ing.); 2004–2009 editor-in-chief of the magazine *Zuschnitt*; 2010–2013 managing director of the HDA Haus der Architektur, Graz; board member of the Austrian Architecture Foundation; freelance author and publisher's representative, publisher and editor; publisher at diachron.

Hisae Hosoi (Ipoh, Malaysia) b. 1933; studied social sciences at the Hosei University in Tokyo, master's degree in 1961. From 1976, Director of the Eishin Board for Financial Management and responsible for the planning and construction of the new campus in Iruma-shi, Saitama Prefecture, with Christopher Alexander; Chairman of the Eishin Board in 1994. In the 1980s and 1990s, numerous articles in magazines and journals, among others, in *Asahi Shinbun, Sanrin, Nikkei Architecture, Jyuutaku Kenchiku*, as well as frequent lecturing at conferences and seminars in Japan from 1985 to 1987, with the emphasis on timber construction.

Gabriele Kaiser (Vienna) b. 1967; studied art history (Mag. Dr. phil.); freelance architectural journalist, exhibition curator and author of numerous articles on Austrian architecture after 1945; 2001–2010 curator at the Architekturzentrum Wien; 2010–2015 director of the afo architekturforum oberösterreich; since 2009 lecturer at the University of Art and Design Linz; board member of the Austrian Society for Architecture (ÖGFA); publisher at diachron.

Christian Kühn (Vienna) b. 1962; studied at the Vienna University of Technology and the Swiss Federal Institute of Technology (ETH) Zurich (Dipl. Ing. Dr.techn.). Teaching at the Vienna University of Technology since 1989. Habilitation in building theory and design, professor at the Vienna University of Technology since 2001. Chairman of the Austrian Architecture Foundation since 2000. Research stay in Japan 2003 ("Temporality and Change in Japanese Architecture"). Member of the OECD Working Group on Educational Building 2005–2011. Dean of the Architecture and Spatial Planning Faculty since 2008. Chairman of the Advisory Council for Building Culture at the Federal Chancellery since 2015. Research areas: history and theory of architecture, building theory with a focus on educational construction. Commissioner for the Austrian contribution to the Architecture Biennale in Venice 2014: *Plenum. Places of Power*. Architecture journalist and critic for daily newspapers such as *Die Presse – Spectrum* and *Salzburger Nachrichten,* as well as in specialist magazines such as *architektur.aktuell, ARCH+, Architektur und Bauforum* and *Merkur;* publications include Hermann Czech, *a+u 554,* 2016:11; *Plenum. Orte der Macht.* (*UmBau 27* Special Edition Biennale Venice), 2014; *Ringstraße ist überall – Texte über Architektur und Stadt,* 2008; *Anton Schweighofer – Der stille Radikale,* 1999; *Das Wahre, das Schöne und das Richtige. Adolf Loos und das Haus Müller in Prag,* 1989.

Claudia Mazanek (Vienna) b. 1951; studied philosophy, political science and social and economic history (Dr.phil.); worked for many years at the Viennese Löcker Verlag (German publisher of Christopher Alexander's *A Pattern Language – Eine Muster-Sprache; The Linz Café);* since 1994 freelance editor and publisher in the field of architecture and art of the 20th and 21st centuries; publisher at diachron.

Norihito Nakatani (Tokyo) b. 1965; Professor at the Department of Architecture, Waseda University Tokyo; architectural historian with a broad range of research interests, including the study of writings on early modern era carpentry, studies on the "Theory of Pre-Existence;" supervisor of a project on the Japanese "Modernist" Kon Wajiro – *A Survey Revisiting the Anonymous Houses from Wajiro Kon's Nihon no Minka;* currently conducting studies on millennium villages in East Asia (http://mille-vill.org). Establishment of "acetate," an editorial and publishing initiative. Publisher of the Japanese translation of Adolf Loos's *Spoken into the Void,* 2012. His own book publications are, among others, *Moving Earth and Shape of Houses: Travelling along the Edge of Eurasia Plate,* 2017, *Revisiting Kon Wajiro's 'Japanese Houses,'* 2012, *Severalness+: The Cycle of Things and Human Beings,* 2011. Awards include the Kon Wajiro Award of the Japan Society of Lifology and the Writer's Award of the Architectural Institute of Japan, 2013.

Hajo Neis (Berkeley) b. 1947; architect and urban researcher. Studied sociology, architecture and urban planning in Frankfurt, Darmstadt, Edinburgh and Berkeley (Dipl.Ing./MCP/MArch/PhD.) Teaches "Urban Architecture, Urban Design and Regeneration." Assistant Professor at University of California 1990–2000, Visiting Professor at the Technical University of Dresden, the University of Applied Sciences Frankfurt, Prince of Wales University Distinguished Teaching Fellowship, Meiji University (Tokyo), University of Duisburg-Essen. Associate Professor at the University of Oregon Department of Architecture since 2001. Director of the Portland Architecture Department for seven-and-a-half years. Founder and director of the Portland Urban Architecture Research Laboratory (PUARL) since 2006, and co-director of the Collaborative for Inclusive Urbanism (CIU). Organizer of international conferences. The main research topic is the further development of *A Pattern Language* and *The Nature of Order* by Christopher Alexander. Board member of the Center for Environmental Structure (CES). Longtime collaborator of Christopher Alexander on numerous projects; project manager of the Eishin Campus. Publications in several languages, including two co-authored books: Alexander, Anninou, King, *A New Theory of Urban Design,* 1987, and Alexander, Moore Alexander, *Battle for the Life and Beauty of the Earth,* 2012.

Ida Pirstinger (Graz) b. 1967; studied architecture at the Graz University of Technology (DI Dr.techn.); until 2007 participation in architecture offices in Graz, Vienna and Salzburg, among others office manager at the architecture office Gangoly; since 2003 teaching at the Graz University of Technology and the University of Applied Sciences Salzburg; 2007–2013 assistant professor at the Institute for Building Structure and Housing Construction Theory of the Graz University of Technology; doctorate in the fields of building theory and urban planning on the densification of inner-city neighborhoods; 2016 research assistant at the Department of Building Physics and Building Ecology at the Vienna University of Technology; since 2014 freelance researcher and consultant; main areas of research: urban development, urban densification, city and building typologies, methodological and typological approaches to sustainable urban development. Board member of IG Architektur. Publications include *Gründerzeitstadt 2.1. Die Nachverdichtung von Gründerzeitquartieren. Ein Modell zur inneren Stadterweiterung,* 2014; *Dense Cities. Materialien zu Schwerpunkten am Institut für Gebäudelehre,* 2013; "Dense Cities. Architecture for Living Closer Together," *GAM.08,* 2012.

Walter Ruprechter (Tokyo/Vienna) b. 1952; studied German philology, history and art history at the University of Vienna; from 1983 to 1985, editor at Medusa Verlag (Vienna/Berlin); 1986 to 1988 lecturer at the German Literature Department of Nihon University in Tokyo; 1989 to 1992 lecturer at the Department of German Studies of Vienna University; 1992–2017 Professor of Literature and Cultural Studies at the Tokyo Metropolitan University, Japan. Years of participation in inter-university projects on questions of cultural exchange, as well as numerous publications. Most recently published: *Passagen. Studien zum Kulturaustausch zwischen Japan und dem Westen*, 2015. Publications also in the field of experimental, avant-garde literature, especially from Austria – Konrad Bayer, Wiener Gruppe, Ernst Jandl, Bodo Hell, etc.

Ferdinand Schmatz (Vienna) b. 1953; writer and poet; studied German language, history, and philosophy at the University of Vienna. 1993–1985 lecturer at the German Literature Department of Nihon University in Tokyo, 1985–1987 lecturer for contemporary literature, at the University of Art and Design Linz; professor since 1988, and head of the Department of "Wordsmithery" since 2012 at the Angewandte (University of Applied Arts) Vienna. Numerous publications (selection): *das gehörte feuer. orphische skizzen,* 2016; *aufSätze! Essays zur Poetik, Literatur und Kunst,* 2016; *Tokyo Echo oder Wir bauen den Schacht zu Babel, weiter,* 2004. Awards (selection): Georg Trakl Preis, Ernst Jandl Preis, H. C. Artmann Preis, Heimrad Bäcker Preis, Literature award of the City of Vienna.

Helmut Tezak (Graz) b. 1948; has been involved with photography since 1976 and has been working since 1981 at the Photographic Laboratory of the Faculty of Architecture, Graz University of Technology. Works (selection): *Dakar,* Graz: Edition Camera Austria, 1984; *Steirisches Weinland,* Graz: Verlag Droschl, 1990; *Chinesisch,* Graz: Verlag Droschl, 1992; *Bilder über Bilder,* 1984–1986, unpublished; *foto. graphisch,* 2004–2012, unpublished. Participations (selection): *Peripherie Graz,* Graz: Haus der Architektur, 1990; *RESOWI,* Graz: Eigenverlag Domenig & Eisenköck, 1996; *GAM.08 Dense Cities,* Vienna: Springer Verlag, 2012; *Werkgruppe Graz,* Graz and Zurich: HDA Graz and Park Books, 2013. Exhibitions (selection): *PHOTOGRAPHs – WHOs,* Forum Stadtpark Graz, 1979; *ArchiGschnas,* Graz University of Technology, 1982; *3Orte,* Neue Galerie Graz, 1987; *Fresh Evidence,* Galerie Marenzi Leibnitz, 2011; *When I Paint My Masterpiece,* Kunstwerkstatt Lienz, 2017.

Takaharu Tezuka (Tokyo) b. 1964; studied architecture at the Musashi Institute of Technology – MIT, Tokyo, and at the University of Pennsylvania; worked 1990–94 at the office of Richard Rogers Partnerships, London; since 1994 he has operated the architecute office Tezuka Architects together with his wife Yui Tezuka in Tokyo; Associate Professor at MIT Tokyo, Visiting Professor at the University of California, Berkeley, the Salzburg Summer University and the Vienna University of Technology; since 2009 Univ. Professor at Tokyo City University. Exhibitions, among others: Venice Biennale 2004, Aichi Expo, Japan, 2005; Nostalgic Future, DAM, Frankfurt/M 2009; Guggenheim Museum, New York, 2010;

JapanLiszt, Raiding, Burgenland, Austria, 2010; Carnegie International, Pittsburgh, PA, 2013. Realizations of single-family homes, schools, kindergartens, hospitals, among others, Fuji Kindergarten, Umbrella House, Deck House, Child Chemo House, Sora no Mori Clinic; projects in New Zealand and the Philippines. Numerous awards and prizes, including Best Kindergarten, OECD, 2011 (for Fuji Kindergarten). Publications, among others: Takaharu + Yui Tezuka, *Architecture Catalogue,* 3 volumes, 2006–2015; *The Yellow Book,* 2016. Videos, among others, Harvard Graduate School of Design, 2013, TED Talk, 2015.

We thank the following sponsors who made essential contributions to making this publication possible:

- Bundeskanzleramt
- Federal Ministry Republic of Austria Europe, Integration and Foreign Affairs

We would like to thank all those who got involved in our project with trust and dedication and provided their expertise: the authors, the interview partners, our photographer Helmut Tezak, the translators Brian Dorsey, Susanne Koppensteiner, Kana Ueda-Thoma, and Ikuo Seo, as well as the designer Margit Steidl.

Moreover, we would like to thank the following persons who contributed significantly to the realization of this book through discussions as well as support during research and travel:

Corina Binder, Architect, Vienna University of Technology
Tomo Furukawazono, Architect, University of California, Berkeley
Sonja Gasparin, Architect, Villach
Eva Heib, Interpreter, Vienna-Tokyo
Wolfgang Heidrich, Librarian, Vienna
Yoko Kitamura, Director of the Eishin Campus, Iruma
Johannes Korherr, Austrian Embassy, Tokyo-Tel Aviv
Gerald Kozicz, Architectural Researcher, Graz
Geraldine Lau, Kimono Specialist, Tokyo-Tel Aviv
Helmut Leitner, Alexander Expert, Graz
Diethart Leopold, Austrian-Japanese Society, Vienna
Mao Matsuda, Photographer, granddaughter of Hisae Hosoi, Tokyo
Takashi Matsuura, English Teacher at Eishin Campus, Iruma
Minami Miyashita, Interpreter, Tokyo
Sockkee Ooi, Architect, Tezuka Architects, Tokyo
Peter Reitmayr, Architect and Japan Traveler, Graz
Konstantin Saupe, Austrian Cultural Forum, Tokyo
Sumie Takazawa, Social Worker and Gourmet, Tokyo

And not least
Christopher and Maggie Moore Alexander, Meadow Lodge, West Sussex, UK

IMPRINT

This book was first published in German by Park Books, Zurich, 2017: *Shifting Patterns. Christopher Alexander und der Eishin Campus.*

Editors
Eva Guttmann, Gabriele Kaiser,
Claudia Mazanek for diachron

Translations
Brian Dorsey (German–English): Guttmann, Kaiser; Beneder; Ruprechter; Kühn; Pirstinger; Appendix

Susanne Koppensteiner (Japanese–English): Nakatani

Kana Ueda-Thoma (English–Japanese): Cover

The Haikus by Ferdinand Schmatz were translated into English by Brian Dorsey, into Japanese by Ikuo Seo.

Copy Editing
Brian Dorsey (English): Hosoi; Neis; Tezuka

Proofreading
Brian Dorsey, Claudia Mazanek

Photographs and Illustrations
Ernst Beneder: 22, 26, 27, 29, 30, 32, 34, 35, 36, 37, 38, 39 / Eva Guttmann: 41 (bottom), 48, 174 / Gabriele Kaiser: 6–7, 15, 21, 40, 48, 49, 160, 165, 176 (bottom) / Gerald Kozicz: 45, 46 (bottom) / Mao Matsuda: 52, 55, 57, 58, 60, 61, 149 (bottom) / Claudia Mazanek: 14 (top), 16, 41 (center), 50, 124, 142, 173 (bottom) / Hajo Neis, CES: 42, 127, 129, 133, 136, 139, 140, 148, 149, 176 / Ida Pirstinger: 151, 153, 157 / Margit Steidl: 44, 126, 138, 156, 173 (center), 174 / Helmut Tezak: 14 (center, bottom), 41 (top), 46 (center, bottom), 63–120, 140 (bottom), 166, 189 / Wikimedia Commons in the public domain: 131, 141 (bottom)

Book Design
Margit Steidl

Typeface
Equitan Sans, Diana Ovezea, 2016
Freishin, Margit Steidl, 2017 (Mutation Freight Text)

Plan Graphic
Gerald Kozicz

Lithography
Elmar Bertsch

Paper
Gmund Color 28, Amber Graphic

Printing
Medienfabrik Graz

© 2019 diachron, Graz, and Park Books AG, Zurich
© for the texts: the authors
© for the images: the photographers

diachron
Association for Disseminating and Deepening the Knowledge about Architecture
www.diachron.at

Park Books AG
Niederdorfstrasse 54, 8001 Zurich, Switzerland
www.park-books.com

Park Books is being supported by the Federal Office of Culture with a general subsidy for the years 2016–2020.

All rights reserved; no part of this publication may be reproduced, stored in a retrieval system or transmitted in any form or by any means, electronic, mechanical, photocopying, recording, or otherwise, without the prior written consent of the publisher.

ISBN 978-3-03860-149-4